CPS
For
Kids

A Resource Book for Teaching

CPS For Kids

Creative Problem-Solving To Children

Bob Eberle & Bob Stanish

PRUFROCK PRESS INC.

ISBN-13: 978-1-882664-26-9
ISBN-10: 1-882664-26-4

Copyright © 1996, Bob Eberle, Bob Stanish

Illustrations by Ginny Bates

Prufrock Press Inc.
P.O. Box 8813
Waco, TX 76714-8813
(800) 998-2208
http://www.prufrock.com

Table of Contents

Something Worth Knowing ...

Since the 1950s the principles and processes associated with creative problem-solving have been researched, refined, taught, and practiced. At the hub of the creativity movement, the Creative Education Foundation has directed its force toward social, physical, economic, emotional, and spiritual well-being. At the vortex of this creative force, the encompassing and well-directed energies of Dr. Sidney J. Parnes and his associates have been evident. How those energies have produced a ground swell of world involvement is a tale of wonder and accomplishment.

Years of Creative Problem-Solving

William Shakespeare considered creative imagination "the gift that makes man the paragon of animals." This pristine power of the human mind has lit lamps, caused scientific discoveries, initiated acts of kindness, and spurred the creation of institutions of progress—including the Creative Education Foundation (CEF).

The Formation of The Creative Education Foundation

The Creative Education Foundation was founded in 1954 by Alex F. Osborn (1888-1966), an innovative advertising executive with a high sense of purpose. Dr. Osborn was seriously concerned about the difficulty and urgency of more fully releasing creativity and problem-solving ability in the individual human being. His keen awareness of a need, and his sincere concern for his fellow man, prompted his pioneering efforts in a relatively little known field.

The formation of the Creative Education Foundation is viewed as a major move to offset the seemingly lack of interest that scholars and social scientists in particular demonstrated toward the field of creativity prior to 1950. In the foreword to his classic book, *Applied Imagination*, Osborn noted that of the 10 leading textbooks on psychology, only a fraction of 1 percent of their cumulative number of pages dealt with creative imagination.

The First Creative Problem-Solving Institute

Applied Imagination stimulated new public awareness of creativity which the book alone could not adequately satisfy. In order to meet public demand, Osborn organized the first Creative Problem-Solving Institute (CPSI) held in Buffalo, NY, in 1955. This highly successful conference attended by approximately 200 individuals, attracted me to the ranks.

New Frontiers

After Osborn's death in 1966, the CEF moved to the campus of State University College at Buffalo (SUCB). With the move came the organization and development of a two-year series of undergraduate courses in creative studies, established by Dr. Ruth B. Noller and me. This four semester course afforded students the opportunity to delve into the nature and nurture of creative behavior and to interrelate their findings with their other studies and experiences.

Interdisciplinary in nature, the creative studies program was made available to stu-

dents in all fields of study. Strong cooperative bonds have been established between this area and the more traditional disciplines such as mathematics, philosophy, and the social and behavioral sciences. Another milestone was realized in 1967 with the establishment of graduate courses in creative studies. Attracting great interest from the onset, the courses ultimately paved the way for the offering of the unique master of science degree in creative studies in 1975. Both graduate and undergraduate programs were placed under the auspices of a newly organized Interdisciplinary Center for Creative Studies (ICCS) in 1976.

Discovery of New Knowledge—Its Integration and Application

The search for new and meaningful knowledge is one of man's greatest continual quests. Thus, it was not surprising that the Creative Education Foundation turned its attention to research in its earliest years. An early step involved investigating the effects of brainstorming on group productivity. Dr. Osborn became intrigued with the ensuing results and provided the basic financial support to launch the CEF's efforts on a more scientific basis. The work that followed is cited among the classic contributions made to the field of creativity research.

The SUCB launched a cooperative effort with the Creative Education Foundation in the form of a Creative Studies Project. The project's goals were to: (1) research the nature and nurture of creative behavior; (2) translate and incorporate the resultant findings into educational programs; and (3) field test programs and disseminate detailed information, first at SUCB, then on a national, and finally on an international, basis. The result was new evidence that the cognitive, divergent, and convergent skills of productive thinking can be successfully nurtured in an educational setting. These findings have had an immeasurable impact on curricula and training programs everywhere, including the annual Creative Problem-Solving Institute.

Dissemination of the most pertinent knowledge in the field has always been a prime thrust of the CEF. From its earliest pamphlets and occasional papers, to its current broad selection of books on creativity, the Creative Education Foundation has served both scholars and the general public as a clearing house for literature in the field. The Creative Studies Library, housed on the SUCB campus, is considered by many to be the most comprehensive special collection of information available in the area of creativity.

The Growing CPSI

Again responding to a need, the institute's objectives were established as:
- to help develop a greater awareness and appreciation of one's ability to be deliberately creative at ever-increasing levels;
- to help develop a strong motivation to utilize one's creative potential;
- to help each one grow in ability to cultivate creativity in others as well as in himself or herself; and
- to help foster and encourage the ideas of others.

Providing for these objectives serves to help increase the probability that participants will experience more and deeper discoveries which will be useful in their per-

sonal and professional lives. This, in turn, helps to increase the number of factors that these individuals will take into account, in a given period of time, while coping with everyday decision-making.

Today, the CPSI curriculum is rigorous and demands considerable individual effort from each participant. "Practice and implementation" has been a much lived-up-to motto of CPSI, for creative education is often likened to physical education. One needs training, instruction in techniques, and plenty of practice in putting it to use.

The CPSI's goals have been translated into action by its thousands of constituents. The growth of the CEF and CPSI is a strong testimonial to a program designed to help people reach a higher level of thought, imagination, and action.

—**Sidney J. Parnes, Ph.D.**
Author, Past President
Creative Education Foundation

Acknowledgments

We are indebted to the many scholars who have contributed to the understanding and application of creative thinking skills. Particularly, we wish to acknowledge the pioneers in the field, including the men and women associated with the Creative Education Foundation.

This work is an outgrowth of the problem-solving techniques developed by the Foundation and taught at the Creative Problem-Solving Institute. With respect, we acknowledge the pioneering contributors to creative problem-solving methodology upon whose shoulders we stand.

Alex F. Osborn, founder of the Creative Education Foundation.

J. P. Guilford, researcher of the structure of intellect theory.

Sidney J. Parnes, president of the Creative Education Foundation (1967-1984).

Ruth B. Noller, chair, CPSI Planning, Faculty, and Program.

Angelo M. Biondi, former director of CEF and editor of the *Journal of Creative Behavior*.

Doris J. Shallcross, pioneering teacher of CPS to high school students.

E. Paul Torrance, pioneering investigator in the cultivation and measurement of creative thinking.

With sincere appreciation, we also acknowledge the educators who served on the panel of reviewers. Their comments and suggestions were most helpful.

Starr Cline	Oceanside, NY
Velma Haslin	Kamploops, B.C., Canada
Bobbie Kraver	Phoenix, AZ
Judy Wooster	Buffalo, NY
Alice Kelley	East Alton, IL
Cindy Allen	Carbondale, IL
Virginia Troutman	Carbondale, IL
Jan Lawrence	Carbondale, IL
Marilyn Hughes	Carbondale, IL
Ralph Litherland	Carbondale, IL

To the Creative Education Foundation and D.O.K. Publishing, we are indebted for their permission to reproduce copyrighted materials.

Preface

Realizing that something needs to be done is a first and necessary requirement for solving problems. The problems of our time, coupled with the need to prepare children to face future challenges, has prompted us to write this book.

This book is especially for:

☞   **Teachers** who believe that problem-solving is one of the more basic skills that can be taught.

☞   **Parents** who are seeking ways to help their children cope with stress in situations which require intelligent decision-making.

☞   **Students** who wish to develop and apply their potential to the fullest for the purpose of solving persisting problems and improving their quality of life.

☞   **Curriculum Specialists and Inservice Training Leaders** who are seeking ways to integrate life application skills with academic programs.

☞   **University and College Instructors** who specialize in the teaching of educational methods courses.

☞   **All Individuals** who face the future with positive convictions that improvement is possible, and that better ways can be found.

—Bob Eberle & Bob Stanish

Foreword

The authors have translated an effective and sophisticated creative problem-solving process into a form which can be learned and enjoyed by elementary school students. Students will find the exercises designed by the authors to be exciting and enjoyable. Their teachers will find adequate information for encouraging and guiding them in mastering and practicing the component skills of creative problem-solving.

As the authors have noted, no single learning prescription fits all students equally well. Practice with these exercises is certain to bring out new stars in the classroom. As we are heading for a new century where co-participation will be imperative, this emphasis in the exercises will be vital in the lives of today's students. The new skills required by the future must be practiced today.

Using several exercises to practice each skill will help students move toward mastery and expertness more rapidly.

The authors have created some alluring exercises—our alligator stayed in our refrigerator nicely when we learned that two fresh pork chops were enticing to him!

—J. Pansy Torrance & E. Paul Torrance
Athens, GA

Part I

Why Creative Problem-Solving for Children?

Introduction
Question:
What skills must children learn to become responsible, contributing, self-sufficient individuals?
Answer:
Because it is the most basic of all skills, problem-solving is a logical and inclusive response.
Question:
How can children be motivated to achieve in the academic subjects?
Answer:
Teaching children how to think and how to apply their thoughts toward a desired outcome is both involving and rewarding to the individual.

Personally, creative problem-solving skills are the tools that allow a child to approach, cope, and deal with social pressures and negative influences. It is significant to note that investigations have shown that the creative thinking processes can be taught to children. When children become more creative, it is not unusual for gains to appear in measures of seriousness, sensitivity, and self-sufficiency. In summary, it can be said that instruction in the creative problem-solving process leads to both cognitive and affective growth in children.

Problem-Solving as a Basic Skill
Psychologist Abraham H. Maslow (1972) has declared, "What a person can be, he must be." Maslow is saying that each person has the need to become all that he or she is capable of becoming. For each child to grow to his or her fullest potential is a wish held by parents and teachers alike. Guiding children along the path to social and academic growth is a monumental responsibility.

Meeting the individual needs of children is a well-established educational goal. It is acknowledged that no single learning prescription fits all children equally well. Yet, an uneasy search for a master plan having general application seems to exist in both home and school. Parents and teachers are expressing the need for a general method, a practical plan for guiding the social and academic growth of children. They are saying that children need to be motivated to grow intellectually and to cope with situations that have no right or wrong answers.

Creative problem-solving is a basic skill and a good sense approach to modern day living and learning. It provides for the application of a broad range of thinking processes. It is a practical style of learning having transfer value. It serves as a model for artistic expression, scientific investigation, and social inquiry. It is also a model for improving relationships, dealing with social uncertainties, and reducing stress that individuals sometimes experience.

CPS in the Classroom

Creative problem-solving is a way of thinking and behaving. When taught in the classroom, it becomes an instructional method for assisting children to become increasingly resourceful, self-sufficient, and productive. Much like other thinking processes, creative problem-solving can be learned, experienced, and applied. However, children will not acquire these skills unless they are taught and practiced. Unlike factual information, CPS skills cannot be found in an encyclopedia.

In practice, CPS follows a six-step method. Each step of the problem-solving scheme has a distinct purpose. As a developmental plan, the six steps are interrelated with one step leading to the next. Teaching and applying the steps as single, self-contained units contributes to simplicity and serves to aid understanding of the over-all scheme. It is for this reason that activities have been prepared for each step or level of the Creative Problem-Solving method. A description of the levels follow. Suggestions for teaching CPS and other implementation tips appear in Part III.

One of the major tasks of the authors has been to modify and adapt established creative problem-solving methods for use with children. In doing so, a serious attempt has been made to view the CPS rational from a child's perspective and experience. It is from this perspective that the six levels of CPS are described.

Stepping The Levels Of
Creative Problem-Solving*

Level I   Sensing Problems and Challenges

Being alert to situations and conditions needing improvement.

Noticing and sensing that things are not as good as they should be.

Level II   Fact Finding

Getting information as an aid to understanding the situation.

Digging in and getting at the cause of things.

Asking questions, finding out about it for sure.

Level III   Problem Finding

Looking at the whole puzzle to see how the pieces fit together.

Using facts to identify the parts of a big problem.

Selecting and stating a manageable problem.

Level IV   Idea Finding

Coming up with lots of ways to solve a problem.

Thinking of ways that are different and far out.

Thinking up things that nobody else will think of.

Level V   Solution Finding

Looking at our ideas to see which one might work.

Coming up with some measures to see how good our ideas really are.

Picking out the ideas that measure out as the best.

Level VI   -Acceptance Finding

Preparing a plan to put our ideas to work.

Figuring out what needs to be done and how to do it.

Finding out about other things that need to be improved.

Note: *The levels appear and should be taught in hierarchical or stair-step order. Each level is an outgrowth of the preceding level and follows in sequential order.*

*The five stage process described by Parnes and his colleagues has been modified for use by children (Parnes, 1967; Noller, Parnes and Biondi, 1976; and Noller, 1977).

Permission to reprint the five stage process appearing in *Scratching the Surface of Creative Problem Solving, A Bird's Eye View of CPS* (Noller, 1977) has been granted by D.O.K. Publishing, Buffalo, NY 14224, and The Creative Education Foundation, Buffalo, NY 14224.

Part II

How Do You Teach Creative Problem-Solving To Children?

Introduction
Question:
In what ways do children learn best?
Answer:
Educational research has given us a wealth of information detailing the characteristics of quality education and the signs of good teaching. These salient factors are listed below.
Question:
Is teaching creative problem-solving different than teaching anything else?
Answer:
If identified characteristics of quality education are accepted as a general mode of instruction, there is no difference. It should be noted, however, that there are certain salient factors (Vincent, 1969) and particular instructional strategies that have direct application to the teaching of creative problem-solving.

Salient Factors
1. *Sensitivity to Situations, Self, and Others.*
   Both teacher and students are alert to emotions which give rise to curiosity, confusion, and conflict. Conscious attention is paid to feelings which suggest that something needs to be done.
2. *Co-Participation.*
   Individuals, as members of the learning group, participate in the making of decisions which involve them. Interaction is supportive, views are shared, and a consensus is reached without coercion.
3. *Individual Initiative.*
   Students are encouraged and opportunities are provided for the initiation of change and improvement. Suggestions for altering the direction of thought and procedure is politely entertained.
4. *Divergent Thinking.*
   Students feel free to engage in imaginative thought and to express uncommon ideas. Imaginative ideas are received without judgement.
5. *Material Facilitation.*
   A variety of resources are available. The creative use and manipulation of materials both in and out of the classroom are encouraged.
6. *Freedom to Learn.*
   Individual expression is encouraged. Opportunities exist for calculated risk-taking; failure is accepted as a learning experience.

Guiding the Group in Brainstorming
Creating, thinking up ideas, is basic to creative problem-solving. For this reason, particular care must be taken in teaching students the techniques of brainstorming

(Osborn, 1961). As an exercise in idea finding, the objective is to produce a large number of ideas which suggest a solution to a problem or challenge. The more ideas the better. Framing the problem statement, saying what you want to gain ideas about, requires exact phrasing. Problem statements appear in the form of open-ended questions which always begin with, "In what ways might we?" or "How might we?" This form of questioning is further described in Level IV activities.

Before each brainstorming session, it is a good idea to review these guidelines:

1. All ideas are acceptable. Don't worry if your idea is good or bad. Don't put people down by laughing at their ideas. Later on we'll decide how good the ideas really are.

2. We like far out ideas. Ideas that are different, wild, and seemingly outlandish may lead us to something really good.

3. Go for a bunch of ideas. The more ideas we have, the better chance we have of coming up with some great ideas.

4. Spin-off of another person's idea. If someone's idea makes you think of another idea, say it. It's OK to combine or build on ideas that have been given.

The brainstorming session should have an opening and a closing. It should occur within an announced time span of three to five minutes in duration, or longer if desired. Brainstorming should not be regarded as an isolated activity. It has a purpose: thinking up ideas that are to be processed and applied to the solution of problems and challenges.

How to SCAMPER for Ideas

Checklisting is a technique often used to stimulate imaginative ideas. The SCAMPER (Eberle, 1996) checklist is an adaptation of the work of Alex F. Osborn (1963). To apply the checklist, simply direct the questioning to the "what ways?" problem statement.

S	Substitute	What could you substitute? What might you do instead? What would do as well or better?
C	Combine	What could you combine? What might work well together? What could be brought together?
A	Adapt	What could be adjusted to suit a purpose or condition? How could you make it fit?
M	Modify Magnify Minify	What would happen if you changed form or quality? Could you make it larger, greater, or stronger? Could you make it smaller, lighter, or slower?
P	Put to Other Uses	How could you use it for a different purpose? What are some new ways to apply it? What does it suggest?
E	Eliminate	What could you subtract or take away? What could you do without?
R	Reverse	What would you have if you reversed it ? Could you change the parts, order, layout, or sequence?

Part III

In What Ways Might I Use This Book?

Introduction
This book has been written and the format designed for busy people. Knowing the authors' intentions and the instructional provisions contained in the book will contribute greatly to its implementation.

Question:
What does this book contain?

Answer:
Six levels of CPS activities, each containing five exercises for student use, provide the content: a total of 30 training activities. It is important to note that each activity is designed to teach the process at the level at which it appears.

A description and overview of each level precedes student activity sheets and serves to acquaint the teacher with the particular processes involved.

Directions for teacher use appear as a separate page and are coordinated with each student activity. The direction page contains: (a) Teaching Target; (b) Introduction; (c) Directions; and (d) Processing information. It should be noted that the words appearing in **bold type** on the teacher's page are identical to those appearing on the student activity page.

Problem-Solving Worksheets may be found in the back of this book. Using the worksheets as guides, the processes taught may be applied to real-life problems.

Instructional Options
Before determining your instructional plan, it is wise to consider the needs, attention spans, interest levels, and developmental progress of your students. Instructional options include:

1. Teaching all five exercises at each level before progressing to the next level.
2. Selecting only those exercises which are meaningful to your students and moving from level to level in progression.
3. Teaching an activity at each level, then applying the worksheets to a class or school problem. Repeat the process using all of the exercises.

When determining your instructional options, apply your own creativity to modify, adapt, or improve on the given information. You may wish to compose activities of your own or even to invite students or parents to compose activities.

Sidney Parnes often says, "Creative Problem-Solving is fun, but it's not for fun." Help your students to understand that CPS is not "fun time." Explain that the exercises are designed to teach them skills that have life-long application. Care should be taken that students do not regard CPS as something cute we do when we have some extra time. CPS is not a late Friday afternoon activity.

It is important that students understand the "Why?" and "What for?" before implementing instruction. Explain that CPS provides a plan for improving things. It helps us

to solve all kinds of problems both at home and school. Be able to suggest some ways in which the students may be able to use CPS after they have learned how to do it.

Before You Start

As a method of thinking and doing, Creative Problem-Solving is best understood and appreciated after the step-by-step processes have been experienced firsthand. The excitement and satisfaction that results from solving problems creatively comes about as individuals learn and apply the processes to challenges that confront them. This is to say that, Creative Problem-Solving methods cannot be fully appreciated by reading about them. Experience is necessary. Those having had formal CPS training will be familiar with the methods contained in this book. However, a review of all sections is recommended.

It is realized that many teachers and parents have not had formal training in Creative Problem-Solving. With this in mind, an easy-to-follow format has been provided. The explanations and instructions are precise. But, something more is needed. Before you start to teach Creative Problem-Solving to children, it would be a good idea for you to have some firsthand experience. The following suggestions provide for both understanding and experience.

Suggestions:

1. Review all sections of this book paying close attention to the explanations given at each of the problem-solving levels.
2. Work some of the exercises at each level. This experience increases in value when a small group of adults work cooperatively to learn and apply CPS methodology.
3. Identify a personal or professional challenge that you face. Then, refer to the worksheet section in the back of the book. Using the worksheets as a guide, apply the step-by-step method to the challenge that you selected. This may be done as an individual or small group activity.
4. Gain further information and improve your instructional sophistication by reading the literature on creativity and problem-solving. Recommended titles appear in the "Bibliography" and "References."
5. Gain proficiency by participating in formal CPS training. For information about the Creative Problem-Solving Institute, write:

The Creative Education Foundation
1050 Union Road
Buffalo, NY 14224
E-mail: cefhq@aol.com

What is a problem?

A problem is ... a toy that you lost.

... when you break something.

... when I get my foot caught in the fence.

... my sister, she bosses me around.

... when you get poison ivy.

... something you don't know what to do about.

... if I don't tell them where I am going.

... getting a green slip (conduct notice).

... when you are all alone and fall and hurt your knee.

... when a tornado comes and blows your house away.

As expressed by first grade students.

Level I

*The solution of problems is the most characteristic
and peculiar sort of voluntary thinking.*
—William James

Sensing Problems And Challenges

Introduction
At times, things get messed up; a toy is broken, a book is lost, a chore is overlooked, an assignment goes uncompleted. Losing a friend, being made fun of, not having time to play, or getting a low grade may be sources of anxiety. It is safe to say that children are not exempt from problems and challenges. Situations that stir the emotions may occur at home, in the neighborhood, or at school. They may range from intense curiosity to total frustration.

Children and Problems
It is not unusual for children to believe that they alone are faced with perplexities. Having things get messed up seems to be something reserved for them. It comes as a mild surprise when children learn that others sometimes experience the same frustrations and anxieties that they experience. To learn that having problems and challenges is not "the end of the world" comes as a satisfying revelation.

Problem Awareness
Sensing problems and challenges is a "peculiar sort of voluntary thinking." The goal is one of becoming increasingly aware of things needing improvement. Progress is made through the realization that things can be better than they are and that something needs to be done. When we sense that something needs to be done, a first step has been taken toward identifying a problem.

Overview of Level I
CPS is a plan, a method for making things better than they are. The outlook is positive, the aim is improvement. Before things can be improved, it is necessary to know that such an opportunity exists.

> **Sensing problems and challenges means that ...**
> you know that something is bothering you.
> the uneasy feeling won't go away.
> you are aware that something is not working out.
> you wish that something were improved.
> you don't know for sure what to do about it.
> you realize that something needs to be done.

Level I activities are designed to provide experiences in sensing problems and challenges. As a result of participating in Level I activities, children will be able to name and describe situations in need of improvement.

Title: Room for Improvement

Teaching Target: To assist students in realizing that almost everything could be made better or done better than it is. To provide a positive focus of finding things in need of improvement as opposed to finding fault. To encourage inventive, creative, and original thought.

Introduction: Has anyone ever said to you, "You have room for improvement"? What were they really saying to you? Having room for improvement means that you need to do something better than you are doing it now. Another way of looking at it is, we all have what it takes to grow and get better at the things we do. That's why you go to school. Today, we are going to check things out and search around the room for improvement.

Directions: From where you are sitting, start at one corner of the room and silently identify everything that you see. As you do this, ask yourself, "Does this thing need to be improved?" If it does, list it in the left hand column. After completing your list, go to the right hand column and answer the question, "Why does it need to be improved?"

Point to the examples and answer questions that may arise. Provide time for the exercise to be completed, then continue.

Look over your list and check one thing that has the greatest need for improvement. Be ready to tell why this thing has the greatest need for improvement and how you might go about improving it.

Processing: Call on students to report on the item they chose as having the greatest room for improvement. Reinforce the notion that almost everything can be done or made better.

Ask students to make a list of the things that they would like to do better. Call it, "My Improvement List."

A second list may be entitled, "I Would Be Happier If ..."

Class discussion may be held on the topic, "My Report Card Says, 'Improvement Needed.'"

Activity #1:   Room for Improvement

From where you are sitting, start at one corner of the room and silently identify everything that you see. As you do this, ask yourself, "Does this thing need to be improved?" If it does, list it in the left hand column. After completing your list, go to the right hand column and answer the question, "Why does it need to be improved?"

What Needs To Be Improved?

Why Does It Need To Be Improved?

Example: The door.

Slams shut when the wind blows.

Example: The chalkboard.

Chalk rubs off on your clothes.

Look over your list and check the one thing that has the greatest need for improvement. Be ready to tell why this thing has the greatest need for improvement and how you might go about improving it.

Title: Chunks in the Ice Cream

Teaching Target: To assist students in sensing and becoming more keenly aware of situations and conditions in need of improvement. To motivate students in seeking out problems and challenges for the purpose of "finding better ways," and "improving things" that condition and influence their lives.

Introduction: How many of you have ever eaten homemade ice cream? Who will tell us about it? Sometimes homemade ice cream has little chunks of ice in it. Have any of you ever found little chunks of ice in your ice cream? What was it like? Did it please you? Finding chunks of ice in your ice cream is an unpleasant surprise. It's not really bad, but it is something you could get along without. It would improve the ice cream if the chunks were not in it.

Directions: Today, we are going to think about things in our lives that we could do without—like "chunks in the ice cream."

Homemade ice cream is one of Ann's favorite things to eat. Sometimes homemade ice cream has little chunks of ice in it, which she really doesn't like. What are some of the things in your life that are like the "chunks of ice in ice cream"?

Write them on the dish of ice cream.

Processing: Given time to respond, students may be asked to talk about the chunks of ice in their lives. Only students expressing a desire to respond should be asked to do so.

Processing questions may include: How many of you feel the same way? Does anyone else experience that same chunk of ice? Do you think that all people have some things that they could live without? Do dogs and cats have little chunks of ice in their lives?

Activity #2: Chunks in the Ice Cream

Homemade ice cream is one of Ann's favorite things to eat. Sometimes homemade ice cream has little chunks of ice in it, which she really doesn't like. What are some of the things in your life that are like the "chunks of ice in ice cream"?

Write them on the dish of ice cream.

Title: It Isn't Fair
_____

Teaching Target: To assist students in realizing that "points of view" and "differences of opinion" are often a source of problems. To bring about an understanding of feelings, attitudes, values, and perceptions as held by themselves and by others.

Introduction: Have you ever heard anyone say: "Try to see it my way," or "I don't look at it that way"? What were they getting at? Can anyone explain what they were saying? It is not unusual for people to have different ideas about things. We say that "everyone has a right to his or her opinion." Do you believe that? OK then, what about when they have an opinion or expectation of what you are supposed to do? How do you feel when somebody tells you, "It's your responsibility," and you don't think it is?

Directions: Responsibilities are things that are expected of us. Parents, teachers, friends, and others expect us to do or accomplish certain things.

Problems occur when there is a difference of opinion between what others expect of us and what we think others should expect of us. When that happens, we often say, "It isn't fair."

First, list things that people expect of you. Take time to do this now. Example: My parents expect me to get all As.

Second, rate each expectation on the fairness scale.

Processing: Call for students to respond and complete the open-ended statement: "I don't think it's fair for my _____ to expect me to _____ because _____."

Ask the questions: Is it fair for parents to have different expectations for their children? Why do you feel that way?

Encourage students to speculate on what causes people to develop expectations of other people.

Activity #3:   It Isn't Fair

Responsibilities are things that are expected of us. Parents, teachers, friends, and others expect us to do or accomplish certain things.

Problems occur when there is a difference of opinion between what others expect of us and what we think others should expect of us. When that happens, we often say, "It isn't fair."

First, list things that people expect of you.

Second, rate each expectation on the fairness scale.

Fairness Scale

Example: My parents expect me to get all As.

	1	2	3	4	5	6	7	
Not Fair								Fair

	1	2	3	4	5	6	7	
Not Fair								Fair

	1	2	3	4	5	6	7	
Not Fair								Fair

	1	2	3	4	5	6	7	
Not Fair								Fair

	1	2	3	4	5	6	7	
Not Fair								Fair

	1	2	3	4	5	6	7	
Not Fair								Fair

	1	2	3	4	5	6	7	
Not Fair								Fair

	1	2	3	4	5	6	7	
Not Fair								Fair

	1	2	3	4	5	6	7	
Not Fair								Fair

If you rated any expectation "4" or below on the "Fairness Scale," chances are that you have identified a problem. The lower the rating, the greater the problem.

Share this page with your parents, teachers, and friends. Talk to them about your responses and listen to what they have to say. Talking it out is a good way to avoid future problems.

Title: The Shape of Things

Teaching Target: To help students to understand that problems are often of a personal nature. What is a problem for one person may not be a problem for someone else. To encourage students to see problems as an opportunity to make things better, to improve things and conditions as they now exist.

Introduction: Raise your hand, but don't answer until you are called on. What shape is a balloon? It could be round or shaped like a hot dog. Could a balloon be flat? If you pressed two books against it, it would be flat on two sides. If we let the air out or punched a hole in it, it would also be flat. When things are going well for us, we kind of float along like a full balloon. At other times, we feel like somebody punched a hole in our balloon. A flat balloon is like a problem. It's not in very good shape.

Directions: Look around you. Everything that you see has a shape.

The things that you see may be round, square, oblong, boy-shaped, or girl-shaped.

Sometimes we talk about people being in "good shape" or "bad shape." Being in "good shape" means that no problems exist. Being in "bad shape" means that there are problems.

Determine the shape of things listed below and place them in the right space.

Processing: Ask, "Is there anyone who has everything in good shape?" If yes, comment that it's good to know that there is someone who doesn't have any problems. If no, comment that it appears that everyone has something to work on.

Continue discussion along the theme that "problems are opportunities to seek improvement in things." Once we find something to be improved we can get busy and do something about it. We can make things better if we really try.

Activity #4: The Shape of Things

Look around you. Everything that you see has a shape. The things that you see may be round, square, oblong, boy-shaped, or girl-shaped.

Sometimes we talk about people being in "good shape" or "bad shape." Being in "good shape" means that no problems exist. Being in "bad shape" means that there are problems.

Determine the shape of things listed and place them in the right space.

A bossy brother or sister.

Being yelled at by parents.

Lost music book.

Getting a bad grade.

A friend being angry with you.

Bent spoke on a bicycle.

Not being invited to a party.

Kids beating you up.

Nothing good to read.

Parents arguing.

Sister or brother does better than you in school.

Add some more of your own if you like.

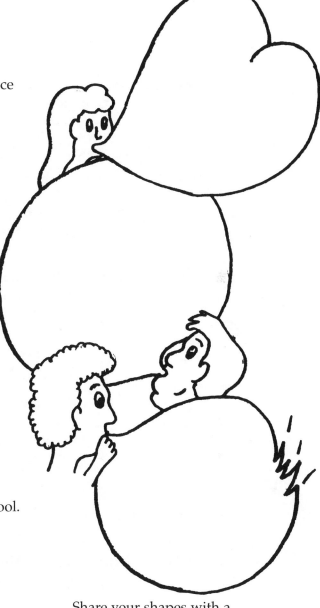

Share your shapes with a friend. Sometimes by sharing problems with others it is possible to get ideas on how to solve them.

Title: Improvement Haystack

Teaching Target: To assist students in sensing and becoming keenly aware of situations and conditions in need of improvement. To encourage students to seek out and identify problems and challenges that exist in their lives. To establish a desire of wanting to improve things that are not quite right.

Introduction: How many of you have ever said, "Give me another chance"? Another chance is an opportunity to do something over in the hope that it can be done better. We all have chances and opportunities to do things better. If we stop to think about it, there are many things that could be improved. Perhaps you can think of some things that could be better at school, at home, on the playground, in the lunchroom, or maybe even with friends. Let's take the time right now to think about things that could be improved.

Directions: An "Improvement Haystack" is a pile of things that could be improved. Let's start by asking the question, **"What needs to be improved?"**

As you think of things that could be better, list them on your haystack.

To get started, we can use the improvement checklist. **Take a word in the first column and join it with a word in the second column. For example, taking the words "friends" and "argument" suggests getting along with my friends.**

As you think of things to improve, start at the bottom and build your "Improvement Haystack."

Processing: Discussion should be guided toward "things that could be done better," rather than "things that are wrong." The idea is to establish a "positive focus" and an understanding that "there are better ways to do things."

Students may be asked, "If you could improve just one thing, what would it be?"

Activity #5:   Improvement Haystack

What needs to be improved?
As you think of things that could be better, list them on your haystack.

Improvement Checklist
Take a word in the first column and join it with a word in the second column. For example, taking the words **friends** and **argument** suggests "getting along with my friends."

family	argument
teacher	helpfulness
friends	appearance
classroom	expectations
schoolwork	anger
pets	understanding
sports	disappointment
money	hopes
my room	responsibility

What is a problem?

A problem is ... something you can't figure out.

... a thing that's hard to solve.

... some kind of trouble.

... when you need help.

... like people calling me names.

... when I don't have anyone to play with.

... when I was watching TV and my mother changed it.

... people teasing me.

... well, it's a problem.

... when older kids pick fights with little kids.

As expressed by second grade students.

Level II

*We can have facts without thinking, but
we cannot have thinking without facts.*
—*John Dewey*

Fact Finding

Introduction

It has been said, "Perception is the guide and controller of behavior." How a person views a situation will determine, to a large extent, what is believed and what will be done about it. The views of a situation may be as many and as varied as the number of viewers. A host of investigations have shown that perception is often faulty. At times, emotions warp our vision. To get at reality, to know the truth of things, other means of gaining information are needed. Fact finding follows the path of scientific inquiry; it seeks to establish reality.

Children and Facts

Due to limited life experience and lack of formal training, children are not prone to look for facts. Stemming from an "I"—"Me" orientation, children are apt to see things from a self-centered point of view. Help is needed if children are to gain rightful information about situations, events, and relationships. Involved is the process of fact finding.

Finding Facts

Finding facts is basic to understanding why a problem exists. The lack of factual information paints an incomplete, distorted picture. With pieces missing it is impossible to see the landscape in its entirety. Helping children is a processing function. The process is one of asking key questions and having children answer them.

Overview of Level II

Having factual data in the information bank makes it increasingly possible to know why things are the way they are. Facts contribute to an understanding of what's going on and why. Fact finding is a skill having immediate and life-long application. It is crucial and basic to all learning.

Fact Finding means that ...
you are checking it out.
you are asking, **why** am I concerned about this?
you are finding out, **what** is involved?
you are determining, **when** is this happening?
you are pinpointing, **where** does this occur?
you are getting at, **who** does this involve?
you are wanting to know, **how** am I, and others affected?

Level II activities are designed to impress children with the need to gain factual information about problematic situations. As a result of participating in Level II activities, students will be able to form fact finding questions about perplexing situations.

Title: The Star Reporter

Teaching Target: To provide instruction and experience which calls for the use of key words in writing fact finding questions. To involve students in a fact finding experience which provides for the organization and application of factual data.

Introduction: Have any of you ever wished or imagined that you were a famous person? Raise your hand if you ever wished to be a: movie star; baseball player; dancer; musician; astronaut; or anything else.

You are a famous person right now, and we want to know more about you. To find out more about you, we will have to ask you some questions. Today, each of you will have the opportunity to do two things: 1) you will be a newspaper reporter and interview a famous person; and 2) you will be a star and answer the questions that the reporter asks you.

Directions: **As a reporter for the *Star*, you are to write a newspaper headline and brief story about a very important person. When you interview the important person you will have to ask good questions. Using the key words given, make up some questions to use when you conduct the interview.**

Let me help you with some examples. You might ask: Who are you? Who do you work for? What made you famous? Or, what is your favorite food? (If help is needed, give examples for the remaining key words.)

Processing: After students have completed their list of questions, form pairs. Instruct students to take turns being the reporter and the person being interviewed. Check to see that answers are being recorded.

When interviews are completed, students may read the headlines and short stories. After reading the stories, the famous people may be introduced to the class.

The opportunity for role playing and other forms of creative expression are limited only by the teacher's imagination.

Activity #6:   The Star Reporter

As a reporter for the *Star*, you are to write a newspaper headline and brief story about a very important person. When you interview the important person, you will have to ask good questions. Using the key words given, make up some questions to use when you conduct the interview.

Fact Finding Question	Interview Answers
Who	
What	
Where	
When	
Why	
How	

Use the facts you have to write a headline and a short story.

_____

The *Star* Reporter

_____

_____

_____

_____

Title: Geni, The Machine

Teaching Target: To provide students the opportunity to apply their power of observation in gathering facts. To encourage students to use facts for the purpose of drawing conclusions.

Introduction: A jigsaw puzzle has many parts. Some of them are very oddly shaped. To piece the puzzle together you have to look carefully at each piece to see where it might fit. After you have finished putting the pieces together, you get the whole picture. To get the "whole picture" of something, we sometimes have to look at the parts.

Today, we are going to look very closely at the parts of a machine. By getting the facts about it, we are more likely to determine its uses.

Directions: This machine is called Geni because it does wonderful things. It works almost like magic. You can't tell for sure what it will do by looking at it, but you can establish some facts.

What are the facts you can determine by looking at Geni? List them in the spaces below. Go over the facts that you have listed. What are some of the things Geni might do?

Processing: Ask students to respond with the facts they have discovered. List them on the chalkboard.

Using the information on the chalkboard as a checklist, have students tell what the machine might do and what characteristics (items on chalkboard) would be used to make it work.

Point out that problems such as: "Who started the fight?" or "Why wasn't homework completed?" might be solved by gathering facts.

What did you learn from this activity that might be helpful to you in solving problems? What are some experiences in your life where looking at the smaller pieces of something would give you a better "picture" than looking at the whole thing? What other ways might observation be helpful?

Activity #7:   Geni, The Machine

This machine is called Geni because it does wonderful things. It works almost like magic. You can't tell for sure what it will do by looking at it, but you can establish some facts.

What are the facts you can determine by looking at Geni? List them in the spaces below.

_____

_____

_____

_____

_____

_____

_____

_____

_____

_____

_____

_____

Go over the facts that you have listed. What are some of the things Geni might do?

_____

_____

_____

_____

_____

_____

_____

Title: **The Fazh**

Teaching Target: To provide students the opportunity to apply their imagination in posing questions that reveal facts. To assist students in realizing that descriptions of things or situations often reveal important facts.

Introduction: Has anyone ever said to you, "Use your imagination"? What did they mean for you to do? We could say that using your imagination means to "think up things." When getting at the facts about something, you have to think up good questions. Today, I am going to ask you to use your imagination to think up some fact finding questions. You will then be asked to answer your questions as if you knew the facts.

Directions: Now that winter was over, Sheri's mother went on her usual spring shopping trip. She bought many things for herself, but she also bought something that Sheri had wanted for a long, long time. Upon returning home, she gave Sheri the Fazh she had been wanting and told her: "All right Sheri, here is the Fazh you have been wanting. Now it's up to you to take care of it. If anything happens to it, it's your fault."

To take care of the Fazh, what will Sheri need to know? Use your imagination to pose questions which get at the facts.

For example: Will it break? Write your fact finding questions below.

Processing: Call on individual students to give their description of a Fazh. Ask for hands to identify the Fazh that has been described. Emphasize that characteristics of things give important facts about them.

Tell about things in your life that are like fazhes, that is, things you have to ask questions about to discover what they are.

Think of some questions that would describe the characteristics of you. Which of these questions would give the most facts?

What are some ways in which you could use your imagination in asking questions? What are some good beginning words for imaginative questions?

 **26 CPS For Kids**

Activity #8:   The Fazh

   Now that winter was over, Sheri's mother went on her usual spring shopping trip. She bought many things for herself, but she also bought something that Sheri had wanted for a long, long time. Upon returning home, she gave Sheri the Fazh she had been wanting and told her, "All right, Sheri. Here is the Fazh you have been wanting. Now it's up to you to take care of it. If anything happens to it, it's your fault."

   To take care of the Fazh, what will Sheri need to know? Use your imagination to pose questions that will get at the facts. For example: "Will it break?" Write your fact finding questions below.

Example: Will it break?

_____

_____

_____

_____

_____

_____

_____

_____

   From the facts that you have established, everyone should know that

a Fazh is _____.

Title: **Tree House**

Teaching Target: To assist students to inquire and ask questions for the purpose of gaining background information about problems that exist. To guide students in building up a store of factual data for the purpose of gaining a more complete picture of what is going on.

Introduction: Sometimes we are at a loss to know why things are the way they are. We say that we are puzzled or confused. We try to figure it out, but we don't get a clear picture of things. Have you ever been puzzled or confused about something? Have you ever said, "I really don't know what's going on?" There are some ways to get the picture of things in clearer focus. The way to do this is to find out the facts of the situation. That's what we're going to do right now, learn how to get facts.

Directions: When Eddie arrived home his mother told him that Joe had stopped by and left a note for him.

Eddie opened the note and became confused about the message. This is what it said:

"Dear Eddie, I am leaving on a vacation with my parents. While I am gone I would like for you to build me a tree house. This drawing will show you how I want it to be built." Allow students time to inspect the drawing.

Before attempting to build the tree house, Eddie will need more information. Eddie will telephone Joe tonight. Write some questions that Eddie should ask to get the facts he needs.

Processing: Role play Eddie's telephone call to you. Have Eddie ask questions and have Joe answer them.

After three or four telephone calls have been role played, ask: "Which of the telephone calls got the most facts?" "Were there enough facts given to build the tree house?"

Close the discussion with, "If you want to get facts, you must ask questions. To solve problems, you need the facts of the situation."

Activity #9:   Tree House

Dear Eddie,

I am leaving on a vacation with my parents. While I am gone I would like for you to build me a tree house. This drawing will show you how I want it to be built.

Your pal,
Joe

Before attempting to build the tree house, Eddie will need more information. Eddie will telephone Joe tonight. Write some questions that Eddie should ask Joe to get the facts he needs to build the tree house.

_____

_____

_____

_____

_____

_____

_____

_____

_____

Title: The Unusual Animal

Teaching Target: To assist students in gaining information by describing or identifying the characteristics of an object or thing. To provide students an opportunity to seek facts for a particular purpose, to solve a problem.

Introduction: Describing something helps us to know more about it. For example, if I asked you to describe your pencil you would look at it and tell what it's like and tell all about it. Who is willing to hold up their pencil and describe it to the class? By describing a pencil, you may have discovered some facts about it that you didn't know before.

Directions: **This is a very unusual animal. What kind of facts can you determine about the animal by looking at its picture? Write them in the spaces below.**

Pretend that you are a zoo keeper and it is your job to keep the animal alive and well. What would you need to know to do this? Ask questions to get the information.

Example: What does it eat?

Processing: Ask children to describe the animal using the information generated in section one. Ask children to give the animal a name and tell why it didn't make it to Noah's Ark. If a child was absent from class at the time of this activity, have him or her draw it on the chalkboard with another child giving the description.

Role play "Zoo Keeper" and "Animal Expert." The "Keeper" asks questions about the animal and the "Expert" gives the answers.

Teacher questions: "How many of you feel that you know this animal rather well?" "Do you like this animal?" "Why do you like or dislike it?" "Would this animal make a good pet?" "Tell why you think so."

Compare characteristics of this animal with others. Select three other animals that would be distant cousins of the *unusual* animal.

Activity #10: The Unusual Animal

This is a very unusual animal. What kind of facts can you determine about this animal by looking at its picture? Write them in the spaces below.

Example: It has a tail like a rat.

_____

_____

_____

_____

Pretend that you are a zoo keeper and it is your job to keep this animal alive and well. What would you need to know to do this? Ask questions to get this information.

Example: What does it eat?

_____

_____

_____

_____

What is a problem?

A problem is ... what I try to keep from happening.

... a thing you can't get rid of.

... something you don't understand.

... my sister, she gets in my way.

... something you have trouble with, it is hard. Dogs and cats have problems, so do people.

... something that bugs you and you can't get your mind off of it.

... when you do something wrong and you think you will get caught.

... when my coach jokes about me and my twin.

... I find a dress that I like, but my mother says it looks like a twenty-year-old dress.

... not having a problem. When people ask, "What is your problem?" you have to say, "I don't have one."

As expressed by third grade students.

Level III

Problem Finding

Introduction

The story is told of a mechanic who charges a thousand dollars for releasing a stuck valve by tapping it with a rubber hammer. When asked to itemize the charges, the statement read: "Ten cents for manual labor, 999\frac{90}{}$ for knowing where to tap." Knowing where to tap is essential to problem-solving. Level III activities, problem finding, helps us know where to tap.

Settling on the Problem

Before settling on the problem to be solved, the problem finding process should be applied. Using a many-directional approach, facts may be reviewed and the problem search conducted. As a result, sub-problems, mini-problems, or contingent problems may surface. When a host of meaningful problem statements is formulated, evaluation follows and it becomes possible to settle on the problem having the greater priority and offering the better opportunity for a creative solution.

Flexible Thinking

Teaching children to find problems involves instruction in flexible thinking. The task is one of assisting students to take detours in thought, to see situations from differing perspectives, and to redefine the challenge presented. When the direction of thought is "detoured," differing scenery comes into view and the problem path may be selected from a variety of routes.

Overview of Level III

Problem finding is a move up on the cognitive ladder. The skills of both analysis and synthesis are involved. When high level thought processes are called for, new stars may appear in your classroom. Likewise, some of the usually bright children may have difficulty functioning at the higher levels of thought. Having a wealth of information, and being asked to do something with it, may be confusing to some children. For this reason, special assistance should be provided to children who experience mental mix-ups.

Problem Finding means that ...
you review your facts.
you view the situation from many angles.
you realize that there may be more than one problem.
you identify sub-problems.
you see the relationship and priority order of sub-problems.
you get at a meaningful, manageable problem.
you open the door to an imaginative production of ideas.

Level III activities are designed to provide experience in analyzing and ordering information. Practice in phrasing questions for creative ideation is also provided. As a result of participating in these activities, children will be able to sort out facts and prepare problem statements which lead to the creative solution of problems.

Title: Locked Out

Teaching Target: To encourage students to consider the implications of a problem situation. To provide students with an opportunity to use their imagination in identifying the many sub-problems suggested by the problem situation.

Introduction: Maybe you have heard someone say that, "Bad luck comes in threes." They mean that when something goes wrong you can look for more things to go wrong. It's true, when you have a problem many others things can get "messed up." Let's see how this works.

Directions: The note on the door said, "We will be back in about six hours." As Sally read the note, she remembered leaving her key on her desk. Now she was locked out.

Wanting to get into the house, and being locked out for six hours, is a problem in itself. Many other problems could come up as a result of being locked out. Use your imagination and think of what some of these problems might be.

Here are some examples:

You might get cold.

It might rain.

Your ice cream will melt.

You promised to call Donna.

Now, list some of the problems that you can think of.

Processing: Call on students to share their list of possible problems. Ask, "If you were locked out and had these problems, which one would you try to solve first? Why did you choose that problem to solve first?"

Have students recall "locked out" experiences and the many sub-problems that resulted.

Ask: "Which problem did you solve first and why?"

 **CPS For Kids**

Activity #11: Locked Out

The note on the door said, "We will be back in about six hours." As Sally read the note, she remembered leaving her key on her desk. Now she was locked out.

Wanting to get into the house, and being locked out for six hours, is a problem in itself. Many other problems could come up as a result of being locked out. Use your imagination and think of what some of these problems might be.

Examples:
I might get cold.
It might rain.
My ice cream will melt.
I promised Donna I would call her.

Now, list some of the problems that you can think of.

_____

_____

_____

_____

_____

_____

_____

_____

Title: What Happened?

Teaching Target: To cause students to view problem situations from the broadest possible perspective. To assist students in recognizing the many sub-problems that might contribute to a problem situation.

Introduction: A baseball coach has to consider many things in picking members for his team and deciding what positions they will play. He needs to think things through and come up with reasons for his decisions. Today, I am going to ask you to think things through, like a baseball coach, and come up with some reasons.

Directions: Members of Scout Troop 34 agreed to meet in City Park at 8 a.m. to pick up litter. Ronnie was there at 8 a.m. but none of the other scouts showed up. Ronnie waited around for an hour and when nobody came, he went home.

What happened? The litter pick-up did not come off as scheduled.

Use your imagination and list some of the problems that might have caused this situation to occur.

Example: The other scouts decided not to come.

Processing: The reasons listed may be viewed as sub-problems. Listing sub-problems not only provides a choice or avenue of attack. It also narrows the problem to a manageable or workable size.

Students are then asked to place a priority on their choices.

When Ronnie got home he decided to find out what happened. Looking at your list, number the problems in the order you believe Ronnie should check them out.

How do you feel when a problem occurs and you are not sure about the cause? List words that would describe these feelings.

In what ways is it better to look at all of the possible sub-problems within a problem?

Recall experiences when a problem occurred and the cause or causes weren't what you originally thought?

Activity #12:   What Happened?

Members of Scout Troop 34 agreed to meet in City Park at 8 a.m. to pick up litter. Ronnie was there at 8 a.m. but none of the other scouts showed up. Ronnie waited around for an hour and when nobody came, he went home.

What happened? The litter pick-up did not come off as scheduled. Use your imagination and list some of the problems that might have caused this situation to occur.

Example: *The other scouts decided not to come.*

_____

_____

_____

_____

_____

_____

_____

_____

_____

When Ronnie got home he decided to find out what happened. Looking at your list, number the problems in the order you believe Ronnie should check them out.

Title: Doubting Debbie

Teaching Target: To encourage students to give thought and consideration to situations that pose problems. To provide students with the opportunity to follow many directions of thought in dealing with a problem.

Introduction: There are times when we find ourselves in troublesome situations. We really don't know what to do. It may be that we did something that caused a problem, or it may be that something just turned out that way.

When we don't know which way to turn, when things seem to be more than we can deal with, it helps to stop and think things through. Today, you will have a chance to think things through and identify some problems.

Directions: Debbie would really like to have Marsha as a friend. Marsha has invited Debbie and several other girls to a party at her house. Debbie knows that some of the girls invited smoke cigarettes and that she would be expected to smoke if she went to the party. Debbie has never smoked and doesn't want to start. She has some doubts about going to the party.

If Debbie goes to the party, or if she decides not to go to the party, there could be some problems.

What problems could come up if she decided to go?

Example: They would laugh at her if she didn't smoke.

What problems could come up if she decided not to go?

Processing: Go back and check over your list of problems. Call for a show of hands. **Should Debbie go to the party? Depending on your answer, which problem will provide the greatest challenge for Debbie?** Call for individual responses.

38 **CPS For Kids**

Activity #13: Doubting Debbie

Debbie would really like to have Marsha as a friend. Marsha has invited Debbie and several other girls to a party at her house. Debbie knows that some of the girls invited smoke cigarettes and that she would be expected to smoke if she went to the party. Debbie has never smoked and doesn't want to start. She has some doubts about going to the party.

If Debbie goes to the party, or if she decides not to go to the party, there could be some problems.

What problems could come up if she decided to go?

Example: They would laugh at her if she didn't smoke.

_____

_____

_____

_____

What problems could come up if she decided not to go?

_____

_____

_____

_____

Go back and check over your list of problems. Should Debbie go to the party? Depending on your answer, which problem will provide the greatest challenge for Debbie?

_____

_____

_____

Title: The Jumping Frog

Teaching Target: To engage students in sequential thinking leading to the identification of sub-problems. To assist students in understanding the need to approach a global type problem through a series of sub-steps or sub-problems.

Introduction: If I gave each of you a wish, what would it be? An example might be: better grades, a new ball glove, more friends, to visit Disney World, etc. (Write some of the wishes on the chalkboard.)

A wish is an expression of "what we want to have happen." Usually, wishing doesn't make things happen. If we want something to happen, we have to do something about it. Doing something about it means we will have to decide on things that we need to do to get our wish.

Directions: **A frog may have to jump on a lot of lily pads to get where it wants to go. Our goals, what we want to have happen, are sometimes like that, too. On the big lily pad, No. 4, write one thing that you would like to have happen.** (Make reference to the example on the left side of the page.) **Now go back to the other lily pads and write what must happen before you get to the big lily pad.**

Processing: Call on students to share their work. This may be done best by having them state their "big goal" and then going back and stating the "smaller goals" in sequential order. By asking students to check on "what comes first" and "what comes next," it can be expected that a lively discussion will follow.

Tell about a problem you solved by taking one step at a time.

In what ways would knowing the smaller goals of a big goal be worthwhile?

Activity #14: The Jumping Frog

A frog may have to jump on a lot of lily pads to get where it wants to go. Our goals, what we want to have happen, are sometimes like that, too. On the big lily pad, No. 4, write one thing that you would like to have happen. Now go back to the other lily pads and write what must happen before you get to the big lily pad.

No. 1: Get a job.

No. 2: Save some money.

No. 3: Shop around for a good buy.

No. 4: Select and buy a new bicycle.

No. 1:

No. 2:

No. 3:

No. 4:

Title: The Great Improvement Machine

Teaching Target: To provide instruction and experience that will assist students in phrasing problems for creative attack. This involves the restatement and narrowing of the problem into sub-problems of workable size.

Introduction: Wouldn't it be great if each of us had a "Great Improvement Machine"? If we wanted to know how to improve something, all we would have to do is write a question on a card and slip it into a machine.

That sounds great, but there's a catch to it. To get good answers from an improvement machine, you have to ask good questions. It's not as easy as it sounds, but let's work on it and see what we can do.

Directions: I'll read the directions. **Before using the Great Improvement Machine, you must complete an improvement card. Below is a sample card. Read what it says.**

(Note: Refer to sample card on activity page.)

Notice that all of the questions begin with: "How might we ... ?" or "In what ways might we ... ?" By asking questions like this, the machine will give back many possible answers rather than just one.

Now, complete your own improvement card. Write what you want to improve in the space provided. Then list your questions.

Remember to start your questions with:

How might we ...   In what ways might we ...

How might I ...   In what ways might I ...

Processing: Using the brackets in front of the question numbers, have students check the question they believe will produce the most useful information. Have students read their question and tell why they selected it.

Close with the following comment: "Each of us really has a great improvement machine, but that's not what we call it. What do we call it, (mind, brain, head)? Remember, if we ask our machine good questions, it will give us many answers to choose from."

 **CPS For Kids**

Activity #15:   The Great Improvement Machine

Before using the Great Improvement Machine, you must complete an improvement card. Below is a sample card. Read what it says.

Sample Card:

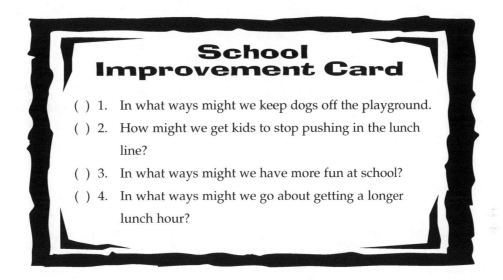

Now complete your own improvement card. Write what you want to improve in the space provided. Then list your questions.

What is a problem?

A problem is ... a thing that you have to work out.

... when people don't like other people.

... to decide if you should tell the truth.

... when someone gets confused.

... something that discomforts you. Love is a big problem.

... it is something you sit and think about, but the answer is hiding somewhere. You walk around and pace the floor and suddenly your answer comes and you don't have a problem anymore.

... trouble. When you have a problem you are usually hurting inside. Life is full of problems, but then a problem can be solved. I've had lots of problems in my life. A problem isn't that bad.

... something you have to get advice about.

... when you want to buy something for ten cents and you only have five cents.

... my report card.

As expressed by fourth grade students.

Level IV

The best way to have a good idea is to have lots of ideas.
—Linus Pauling

Idea Finding

Introduction
Sometimes referred to as divergent thinking, applied creativity leads to the production of unique and useful ideas. Creative ideas flower inventions, compositions, and solutions to complex problems. The late Alex F. Osborn often spoke of "accelerating our imagination" by implementing certain techniques. Two of these techniques are described in Part II under the titles: "Guiding the Group in Brainstorming" and "How to SCAMPER for Ideas." It is recommended that these be reviewed and applied when teaching Idea Finding. (See pages 4–5.)

A Basic Concept
Idea Finding, as applied to CPS is a basic concept. Generating creative ideas is the difference between CPS and other forms of problem-solving. Brainstorming places an emphasis on an all-out drive for a large number of possible solutions to problems. Often misunderstood, the production of a large number of ideas is not the sole function or the end result of brainstorming. Wild ideas must be tamed and made functional. New ideas need to be created by combining and spinning off of existing ideas. All ideas need to be worked, reworked, and modified.

Suspending Judgement
Divergent thinking and convergent thinking are two distinct mental operations. Thinking up ideas and evaluating ideas are also two distinct functions and should not be applied at the same time. When producing ideas, suspend judgement. The worth of the idea can be determined later. All ideas are acceptable.

Overview of Level IV
As a creative pursuit, Idea Finding may incorporate most, if not all, of the thinking processes associated with imaginative productive thought (Torrance, 1962). Included are four of the more common modes of thinking associated with creativity.

Fluent Thinking ——————→ generating a number of ideas or answers.
Flexible Thinking ——————→ moving to contrasting categories.
Elaborate Thinking ——————→ embellishment, adding great detail.
Original Thinking ——————→ a unique, one of a kind, response.

Idea Finding means that ...
you produce a large number of ideas.
you give your ideas an unusual or unexpected twist.
you spin off of other ideas and combine ideas to see what will happen.
you suspend judgement and let all ideas surface.
you work and rework your ideas to give them greater meaning.

Level IV activities are designed to provide experiences in generating creative ideas. As a result of participating in these activities, students will be able to increase the number of ideas generated in a given period of time and will improve the quality of their ideas toward originality and inventiveness.

Title: The Thing

Teaching Target: To encourage students to use their imagination. To provide students with the opportunity to produce creative ideas.

Introduction: How many of you have ever said, "I've got an idea"? Saying that suggests that you were looking for a way to solve a problem.

When you shared your idea with others, has anyone ever said, "That's dumb" or "It won't work"? New ideas sometimes sound crazy, but remember, far out ideas often suggest ways to solve real problems. Let's find out how many far out ideas you can come up with.

Directions: **A wild inventor has created "The Thing," but he doesn't know what it is to be used for. Let's help the inventor by thinking of some uses for "The Thing." Make your ideas as wild as his invention.**

"The Thing" might be used to:

Examples:

Boot kids that cause trouble.

Stomp the floor and scare burglars.

Continue with the second section after providing time for the first.

Are there any of your ideas that can be combined to create a new idea? Write them down.

Processing: Ask students to count their ideas. Ask those with the most ideas to share them. Call for ideas that have not been mentioned. Call for a combination of ideas.

Impress upon students that wild ideas may not have value until we "work them over." When we take wild ideas and "work them over," we can often come up with ideas that help us solve problems.

What are some things that have uses other than their intended use? Think of two things that, if combined, will produce a new use. Think of things in stores which represent a combination of uses. Discuss how wild ideas might be put into practice.

Activity #16: The Thing

A wild inventor has created "The Thing," but he doesn't know what it is to be used for. Let's help the inventor by thinking up some uses for "The Thing." Make your ideas as wild as his invention.

"The Thing" might be used to:
Examples:

Boot kids that cause trouble.

Stomp the floor and scare burglars.

_____

_____

_____

_____

_____

_____

_____

_____

_____

Are there any of your ideas that can be combined to create a new idea? Write them down.

_____

_____

_____

_____

Title: Sammy's Secret

Teaching Target: To convey the idea that creative ideas have application in person-to-person relationships. To encourage students to generate unique, one-of-a-kind solutions to problems.

Introduction: When we become confused and don't know for sure what to do about something, we say that we have a problem. When something stands in our way and keeps us from doing what we want to do, we say we have a challenge. When there is a chance of doing something good, or making things right, we say that we have an opportunity.

In meeting, working with, or just being with other people, we often have problems, challenges, or opportunities. Creative ideas can help us in dealing with "thing" problems. They can also help us in dealing with people problems.

Directions: **Sammy gets good grades because he gets the test questions right. He seems to know what the questions will be ahead of test time. When asked about it, Sammy says, "Yep, I have a secret way of knowing what the questions will be." You would like to get good grades on the tests, and you would like to know Sammy's Secret. Can you figure out how to get Sammy to share his secret?**

Answer the question: "How might I get Sammy to share his secret with me?" List all the ways you can think of.

> **Example: Tell Sammy that he is a "good" kid and should share his secret.**

List some ways that nobody else will think of.

Processing: Have someone play the role of Sammy. When ideas are addressed to Sammy, he responds with a "thumbs-up" to indicate that he might share his secret. "Thumbs-down" indicates that he won't share his secret. Sammy may be asked to tell why he gives a "thumbs-up" or a "thumbs-down."

Was this a good activity to do? In what ways might this experience help you in getting to know and understand people? Will knowing what you learned here make you a better person? In what ways?

 **48 CPS For Kids**

Activity #17: Sammy's Secret

Sammy gets good grades because he gets the test questions right. He seems to know what the questions will be ahead of test time. When asked about it, Sammy says, "Yep, I have a secret way of knowing what the questions will be." You would like to get good grades on the tests, and you would like to know Sammy's Secret. Can you figure out how to get Sammy to share his secret?

Answer the question: "How might I get Sammy to share his secret with me?" List all the ways you can think of.

Example: Tell Sammy he is a "good" kid and should share his secret.

_____

_____

_____

_____

List some ways that nobody else will think of.

_____

_____

_____

_____

_____

_____

Title: **Alligator in the Refrigerator**

Teaching Target: To provide students with the opportunity to develop unique ideas to solve a strange problem. To encourage students to be inventive in their production of ideas.

Introduction: Being responsible for something or somebody places us in the position of performing a duty. We are expected to do something because we are being counted on to do it. Do any of you have responsibilities or duties? Will you share them with us? Our pets depend on us to provide for them. Looking out for our pets is not too difficult unless you have a strange pet.

Directions: **Your pet alligator has become very ill. You don't know what to do, so you call the veterinarian. The veterinarian tells you that if your pet is to survive you will have to lower his body temperature 20 degrees centigrade. The only thing you can think of is to put the alligator into the refrigerator. With no one home to help you, you have a problem of putting a large, snapping animal into the refrigerator.**

In what ways might I put the alligator into the refrigerator? List all the ways that you can think of.

Example: Put a frog in the refrigerator and the alligator will jump in after it.

We have not given the alligator a name. What name would you give the alligator? Give it a name no one else will think of.

Processing: When asking students to share their ideas, remind them all ideas are welcome. It is not the purpose of sharing to determine which ideas are good and which ones are not. Right now, the search is for a lot of ideas. Wild ideas are welcome.

Describe in more detail how some of your ideas might work. Can you combine any of the ideas to arrive at some new ideas?

Are there any ideas that could be drawn or illustrated more easily than written? In what ways is the name you gave the alligator an appropriate or good name for him?

Activity #18: Alligator in the Refrigerator

Your pet alligator has become very ill. You don't know what to do, so you call the veterinarian. The veterinarian tells you that if your pet is to survive you will have to lower his body temperature 20 degrees centigrade. The only thing you can think of is to put the alligator into the refrigerator. With no one home to help you, you have a problem of putting a large, snapping animal into the refrigerator.

In what ways might I put the alligator into the refrigerator? List all the ways you can think of.

Example: Put a frog in the refrigerator and the alligator will jump in after it.

_____

_____

_____

_____

_____

We have not given the alligator a name. What name would you give to the alligator? Give it a name no one else will think of.

_____

Title: **My Name Smelz**

Teaching Target: To encourage students in the fluent production of ideas that would provide possible solutions to personal problems. To encourage students to react rationally when faced with disturbing situations.

Introduction: "Sticks and stones will break my bones, but names will never hurt me." Have any of you ever heard that before? What does it mean to you? Do you believe that it's true that "names will never hurt you"? Our activity today deals with name calling. Perhaps we may find some ways to deal with this problem.

Directions: Just suppose that your last name was Smelz. As you might guess, there would be some people who would make fun of your name. To be called "smelly" or "stinky" bothers you, and you want to do something about it. What might you do about it? Find answers to the question: "How might I stop people from making fun of my last name?" List all the ways you can think of.

Example: Fight them, give them a good punch.

Go far out and complete the page with some "wild ideas" that just might work.

Processing: First, call for sharing of ideas written above the "Go far out and complete the page" line. Then call for ideas from the lower section of the page. Ask students to compare the ideas. Ask, "Did they seem to be different?" Help students to see that "the more ideas you have, the better the chance for a really new creative idea."

How might "wild ideas" be helpful?

Describe some problems that are worse than name calling.

Tell about a time in which you could have used a lot of ideas.

What did you learn from this activity? In what ways will it be useful? Was this activity a good thing to do?

Activity #19: My Name Smelz

Just suppose that your last name was Smelz. As you might guess, there would be some people who would make fun of your name. To be called "smelly" or "stinky" bothers you and you want to do something about it. What might you do about it? Find answers to the question: "How might I stop people from making fun of my last name?" List all the ways you can think of.

Example: Fight them, give them a good punch.

_____

_____

_____

_____

Go far out and complete the page with some "wild ideas" that just might work.

_____

_____

_____

_____

_____

_____

Title: Danny and His Friends

Teaching Target: To involve students in a real-life problem-solving situation. To cause students to stretch their minds in search of problem-solving ideas.

Introduction: If your basketball team was behind by one point and you had two free throws, how hard would you try? Tell us how you would go about it. Solving problems is like trying to make free throws. You really have to try. If you don't want to try, you can just pretend that the problem will go away. Do you think that problems usually go away by themselves without anybody doing anything about them? Here is a problem that won't go away. In fact, it could get worse.

Directions: Danny and five of his friends decided to go to the corner drugstore. On the way, Bill tells Danny, "It's your turn to steal something from the store." The other boys offer suggestions like stealing candy bars or comic books.

Danny knows it's wrong and doesn't want to be involved in stealing anything. He wants to keep his friends but doesn't want to get into trouble. Danny has a problem.

Let's get some ideas to help Danny solve his problem. What might Danny say or do to convince his friends that stealing at the drugstore is the wrong thing to do? List all of the ideas you can think of.

Example: Tell them that he has some money and doesn't have to steal anything.

After providing them time to list ideas, say:

Now go back and check the three ideas that you feel have the best promise for solving the problem. Be prepared to tell why you think they are the best ideas.

Processing: Discussion should center on the ideas that seem to be convincing. Student responsibility for their behavior and the consequences of stealing should be mentioned. Care should be taken to avoid discussions about stealing which involve class members.

How might this activity be helpful in other situations? Was this activity worth doing? What makes problems of this type difficult to solve?

Activity #20: Danny and His Friends

Danny and five of his friends decided to go to the corner drugstore. On the way, Bill tells Danny, "It's your turn to steal something from the store." The other boys offer suggestions like stealing candy bars or comic books.

Danny knows it's wrong and doesn't want to be involved in stealing anything. He wants to keep his friends but doesn't want to get into trouble. Danny has a problem. Let's get some ideas to help Danny solve his problem. What might Danny say or do to convince his friends that stealing at the drugstore is the wrong thing to do?

List all of the ideas you can think of.

Example: Tell them that he has some money and doesn't have to steal anything.

_____

_____

_____

_____

_____

_____

_____

Now go back and check the three ideas you feel have the best promise for solving the problem. Be prepared to tell why you think they are the best ideas.

What is a problem?

A problem is ... a thing you must solve to reach a goal of some sort.

... something that bugs you and you can't seem to escape.

... when someone hurts your feelings.

... when your mind gets all mixed-up.

... something to overcome. It is something that fights you and you have to fight back. It comes in many forms and is always with you.

... something you have to solve so you can feel better.

... not being able to think of a design for hooking a rug.

... trying to be nice to my little sister when I really want to scream at her.

... my mom and dad, they fight all the time.

... getting people to pay me back when I lend them money.

As expressed by fifth grade pupils.

Level V

*No idea is so outlandish that it should not be considered
with a searching but at the same time, with a steady eye.*
—*Winston Churchill*

Solution Finding

Introduction

The stage level progression of creative problem-solving leads to the application of "the higher level" thinking skills. Appearing at the upper reaches of taxonomical models, stage levels of development, and educational objectives, these skills become increasingly complex and intellectually demanding. Contrary to developmental theory, investigations have shown that upper level, complex intellectual skills can be understood and applied by elementary school children.

Valuing and Evaluating

It is necessary that a distinction be drawn between valuing and evaluation skills. The former, an affective expression, involves personal choice, likes, attitude, and beliefs. It is an expression of preference. In contrast, evaluation is judgement based on evidence, criteria, or established standards. The conclusions reached as a result of evaluation tend to be logical, reasonable, and relevant. Evaluation is a scientific approach to decision-making.

Promise of Success

Applying evaluation techniques provides the opportunity to judge potentially promising ideas against each other. This is done by applying evaluative criteria to ideas to determine their comparative usefulness. The end result of solution finding yields information which indicates a promise of the successful solution of the problem.

Overview of Level V

Solution finding calls for the application of both divergent and convergent thinking skills. Once promising ideas have been selected, it becomes necessary to conduct a comparative evaluation. Divergently, evaluative criteria are produced. Convergently, the evaluative criteria are applied and the narrowing process conducted. It is through this activity that the most promising solution may be found.

Solution Finding means that ...

you remain emotionally apart from your ideas.
you produce measures to evaluate your ideas.
you have data to support your choice of ideas.
you look at ideas realistically.
you consider more than one course of action.
you select an idea that has the best chance of succeeding.
you are not afraid to make a decision.

Level V activities go beyond the "like" or "dislike" method of decision-making. Solution finding involves the use of analysis, synthesis, and evaluative skills. As a result of participating in Level V activities, students will be able to generate and apply evaluative criteria for the purpose of finding promising ideas.

Title: The Ideal Candy Bar

Teaching Target: To provide students an experience in generating descriptive criteria. To create an awareness and understanding of characteristics and qualities as evaluative measures.

Introduction: Write the words "Biggest" and "Best" on the chalkboard. For each, call for words meaning about the same and list them. Continue discussion by asking students to make a choice: "Those preferring things that are best, raise their hands." Call on students to defend their choices. Close discussion by pointing out the biggest is not always the best. Size and quality are not the same standards of measurement. In our activity today, we will deal with size and quality.

Directions: **Your teacher has asked everyone to listen closely for a surprise announcement. When the class becomes quiet, this is what she says, "A company that makes candy bars has asked for our help. It plans to make an ideal candy bar. Any student who can ask twelve questions about candy bars will get a free box."**

Questions about the candy bar:

Example: Does it have peanuts?

Processing: Taking turns, call for students to share their questions. List questions on the chalkboard under the appropriate headings such as size, quality, and cost. Close discussion by clinching the point that these words indicate "standards" which may be used to judge things.

If you were a judge whose job it was to pick a name for the new candy bar, which of the questions listed would be most helpful? Check the three that you feel would be most helpful. My name for the ideal candy bar is:

Continue discussion by asking, "How did you arrive at that name? If we were to select the five best names for the candy bar, how would we go about doing it?"

Call for student suggestions. Make a list of standards (evaluative criteria). Show how the standards may be used in selecting the best names.

Activity #21: The Ideal Candy Bar

Your teacher has asked everyone to listen closely for a surprise announcement. When the class becomes quiet, this is what she says, "A company that makes candy bars has asked for our help. It plans to make an ideal candy bar. Any student who can ask twelve questions about candy bars will get a free box."

Example: Does it have peanuts?

1. _____

2. _____

3. _____

4. _____

5. _____

6. _____

7. _____

8. _____

9. _____

10. _____

11. _____

12. _____

If you were a judge whose job it was to pick a name for the new candy bar, which of the questions listed would be most helpful? Check the three that you feel would be most helpful.

My name for the ideal candy bar is: _____.

Title: What's Good About It?

Teaching Talent: To engage students in flexible thinking. To provide experience designed to gain differing points of view. To assist students in discovering that the worth of something is determined by the conditions that are applied.

Introduction: There's an old saying that goes something like this, "Don't judge another person until you have walked in his moccasins." What does that mean to you? Is that a good way to think about things? Why do you feel that way about it? Today, you will have the opportunity to put on someone else's shoes. You will be asked to use your imagination and see different points of view.

Directions: Usually things are not "all good" or "all bad"; it depends on how you look at it. What may be good for one person may be bad for another. To get different points of view, you have to put yourself in another person's shoes, so to speak. To do this you have to use your imagination.

Here's how we play this game: I will read the statement on the left hand side of the page and then give you some time to think about it. Then I will ask, "What's good about it?" After you answer the question, I will ask, "What's bad about it?"

Raise your hand if you wish to answer. Here we go.

Example:

It's raining very hard.   **What's good about it?**
                           Farmers need rain.
                           What's bad about it?
                           It will spoil the picnic.

Processing: What did you learn by playing this game? Was it harder to think up "good things" or "bad things"?

Why is that true?

Activity #22: What's Good About It?

Usually things are not "all good" or "all bad"; it depends on how you look at it. What may be good for one person may be bad for another. To get different points of view, you have to put yourself in another person's shoes, so to speak. To do this you have to use your imagination.

Here's how we play this game: I will read the statement on the left hand side of the page and then give you some time to think about it. Then I will ask, "What's good about it?" After you answer the question, I will ask, "What's bad about it?"

Raise your hand if you wish to answer. Here we go.

Here's an example:

It's raining very hard.
What's good about it?
Farmers need rain.
What's bad about it?
It will spoil the picnic.

	What's Good About It?	What's Bad About It?
It's raining very hard.	Farmers need the rain.	It will spoil the picnic.
Billy was absent today.		
Mary was called to the office.		
Tom lost a quarter.		
Your teacher lost the test.		
The principal played softball.		
The bus was late.		
Lunch prices went up.		
Joe struck out.		
Someone took your bike.		

What did you learn by playing this game? Was it harder to think up "good things" or "bad things"? Why is that true?

Title: Super Shopper

Teaching Target: To build an understanding of "standards" and the use of "criteria" to make judgements. To provide students an experience in developing judgmental standards.

Introduction: Have any of you ever won a "first prize" in anything? What did you do to win a "first prize"? What made you better than the persons who won "second" and "third"? To be judged "first" means that you did something better than the others. Judges usually have a list of things that they check you on. The things they check you on are called "standards." Today, you will be asked to make up a checklist of standards. If you are going to be the judge, you have to have something to check on.

Directions: **You are given the task of going to the store and buying enough groceries for an entire week. As you make up the list of things you will buy, you decide that you want to do an excellent job of buying groceries. You want to be a "super shopper." What does a super shopper do? Make a list of the things you would use to judge super shoppers.**

Example: Use coupons to save money.

Processing: Students should be helped to understand that their list of "standards" may be used to determine "how good" or "how well" people do in their grocery shopping.

Students should also be helped to understand that standards may be developed and used to judge their ideas before putting them to practice.

For a lively discussion, it is suggested that teachers skip around the class calling on hands that are raised. A "master list" may also be written on the chalkboard.

Activity #23: Super Shopper

You are given the task of going to the store and buying enough groceries for an entire week. As you make up the list of things you will buy, you decide that you want to do an excellent job of buying groceries. You want to be a "super shopper." What does a super shopper do?

Make a list of the things you would use to judge super shoppers.

Standards for Judging Super Shoppers

Example: *Use coupons to save money.*

_____

_____

_____

_____

_____

_____

_____

_____

Take your list home and ask the family shopper some "Do you?" questions.
Example: *Do you use coupons to save money?*

_____

_____

Title: Lunch Line

Teaching Target: To provide an experience in evaluating ideas. To reason and project the outcome of ideas if and when they are implemented. To gain experience in defending choices.

Introduction: Write on the chalkboard, "Here's a new word for you: Consequences." Who can tell me what it means? It means that, if you do something now, you can pretty well predict that something will follow. Something else would happen as an outcome. For example: if you came to school late, you would get a tardy mark on your report card. Being marked "late" is the outcome or consequence of not getting to school on time. If you were tardy every day for a whole week, there might be other consequences. What might they be?

It's the same way with ideas, we have to consider the outcome, or consequences, if we follow through with an idea. In considering the consequences, we can judge how good an idea might be. Today, you will have an opportunity to judge some ideas and to list some of your own.

Directions: Suppose that one of the problems in your school is kids pushing in the lunch line. The pushing upsets people, they argue, and eating becomes a hassle. You decide that things could be better, and you want to find ways to improve the situation. So you ask the question: "In what ways might I go about getting kids to calm down in the lunch line?"

Here are some answers. Add some of your own.

Judge each idea using the rating scale. Be prepared to tell why you gave each idea a particular rating.

Processing: Discuss the ratings given to each idea.

Ask, "If you choose to do that, what might be the outcome? What would the consequences be?" What is meant by "hasty" decisions? How might "hasty" decisions be avoided?

Activity #24: Lunch Line

Suppose that one of the problems in your school is kids pushing in the lunch line. The pushing upsets people, they argue, and eating becomes a hassle. You decide that things could be better, and you want to find ways to improve the situation. So you ask the question: "In what ways might I go about getting kids to calm down in the lunch line?"

To rate each idea, circle a number on the 1 to 5 scale.

Idea Rating Scale

	Poor Idea		Fair Idea		Good Idea
1. Talk to the principal about it.	1	2	3	4	5
2. Complain to the lunchroom supervisor.	1	2	3	4	5
3. Hit the kids who cause trouble.	1	2	3	4	5
4. Tell my parents about it.	1	2	3	4	5
5. Write a letter to the newspaper about it.	1	2	3	4	5
6. Threaten to beat up the troublemakers.	1	2	3	4	5
7. Get permission to play records.	1	2	3	4	5
8.	1	2	3	4	5
9.	1	2	3	4	5
10.	1	2	3	4	5
11.	1	2	3	4	5
12.	1	2	3	4	5

Judge each idea using the rating scale. Be prepared to tell why you gave each idea a particular rating.

Title: Idea Report Card

Teaching Target: To provide students with experience in applying evaluative criteria. To gain experience in finding promising solutions to problems.

Introduction: Who is the fastest runner in the class? You may think that you know the answer, but you may not be right. To find out for sure, we may have to have a race and set up some measurement standards. For example, we might ask "Who is the fastest runner for the 50 meter dash? A 100 meter dash? A 400 meter run or a 1600 meter run?" You see, it gets a little complicated. It also gets a little complicated when we attempt to find out which ideas are the best. There are ways to do this. Let's try it right now.

Directions: **Sometimes when things are not going well, or when adults have a headache, we say they are having a bad day. When adults have a bad day, they may become easily upset and sometimes yell at children. To keep from being yelled at too much, you have come up with some ideas. Now it is time to give your ideas a grade to see which ones are the best.**

Refer to Activity #25. Ask students to read along with you as you read the Report Card Rating Scale and the directions for marking the report card. Students may be asked to read the Creative Ideas and the Measures. Provide time for students to mark the Report Card and caution them to award grades across the scale.

Processing: You should ask several questions.

Which one of the ideas got the best report card?

Did anyone have a different winner?

Which of the ideas was second best? Do you agree on the second best idea?

Could you combine them to make an even better idea? Raise your hand if you wish to tell us your combined idea.

Seek student comments on the activity. Ask if anyone experienced some surprises.

Activity #25: Idea Report Card

Sometimes when things are not going well, or when adults have a headache, we say they are having a bad day. When adults have a bad day, they may become easily upset and sometimes yell at children. To keep from being yelled at too much, you have come up with some ideas. Now it is time to give your ideas a grade to see which ones are the best.

Report Card Rating Scale

A - Excellent   B - Good   C - Average   D - Below Average   F - Failure

Starting with measure No. 1, compare all of your ideas across the page. Then, give all of your ideas a grade before going on to measure No. 2. Compare your ideas with measure No. 2, and give them a grade. Continue in this manner until all measures have been given a grade.

How might I stop people from yelling at me?

MEASURES to see how good your ideas are.	Yell back at them.	Skip back-ward around the room.	Offer to get some aspirin.	Pretend to cry.	Hum a happy song.
Example: Will cheer them up.	D	B	A	B	D
1. Something I can do by myself.					
2. Will not take too much time.					
3. Will not make them yell more.					
4. Will last for a while.					

(table header band: **Creative Ideas**)

Which of the ideas was second best?

Could you combine them to make an even better idea?

CPS For Kids 67

What is a problem?

A problem is ... to not know what to do.

... when your mind is all locked up and you try to think of something else, but your mind won't let it come in.

... something you have when things aren't going right.

... a thing that needs a solution and occurs between two parties.

... my braces. We need the money for other things.

... doing homework without knowing how.

... my dog is getting sort of old and when she comes in from the cold she is stiff. I worry about her.

... worrying. I don't think I will get a new bike for my birthday.

... my mother works all the time.

... my way of talking sassy.

As expressed by sixth grade students.

Level VI

Acceptance Finding

Introduction

Strange as it may seem, children are expected to be imaginative and creative, but seldom are their ideas taken seriously. The exceptions being understanding parents who involve their children in family planning and enterprising teachers who capitalize on the ideas of students to organize the day-to-day instructional scheme. For the most part, the ideas of children are taken lightly and unceremoniously squelched. Be they from children or adults, new ideas have the ring of the ridiculous that frequently triggers laughter and put-downs. For this reason, extreme care must be taken in gaining acceptance for new ideas.

Predicting and Organizing

Teaching for acceptance finding involves both prediction and organizational skills. Looking ahead to what might happen, it becomes necessary to predict difficulties and find ways to overcome them. It is also necessary to develop an organizational plan and timetable for moving ahead. The role of the instructor in teaching acceptance finding skills is that of provoker and clarifier. This may be accomplished by posing the familiar Who? What? When? Where? Why? and How? line of questioning. Questions may be addressed to: the involvement of others; gaining enthusiasm; ways to overcome criticism; place or location; resistance to change; pointing out advantages; and detailing the plan for implementation. The question arises, "Is all of this detailed planning and organizing necessary?" The answer is a resounding YES! Acceptance finding is critical to problem-solving. If a good idea cannot be implemented the problem will not be solved.

Overview of Level VI

Acceptance finding causes us to predict what might happen when our problem solution is introduced. It takes into consideration the need for a detailed, step-by-step implementation plan. Acceptance finding is a grand and elaborate effort; it is a general systems flow chart of events; it is a battle plan for winning the war.

Acceptance Finding means that ...

> you know what you hope to accomplish.
> you are getting people to support your idea.
> you anticipate the difficulties that may arise.
> you know what resources will be needed and where to get them.
> you have a step-by-step implementation plan.
> you have a timetable and schedule of events that are to take place.

Level VI activities are designed to provide predicting and organizational skills. As a result of participating in Level VI activities, students will be able to identify and list difficulties that may arise in implementing ideas. They will also be able to prepare a detailed plan for implementing an idea through the application of acceptance finding strategies.

Title: **The Right Order**

Teaching Target: To create an awareness of the need for planning and order in the implementation of an idea. To provide students with an opportunity to "look ahead" and to anticipate the details that may be involved in implementing an idea.

Introduction: Here's a saying that you might, or might not, agree with: "Don't cross your bridges until you come to them." What does that mean? How many of you agree with the idea of "not crossing your bridges"? How many of you disagree? When I call on you, explain why you think the way you do.

Let's see how it might work out if we have an idea that we want to put to work.

Directions: Your neighbor is the manager of a supermarket. When he arrives home for lunch at 11:30 a.m., he tells you that he needs 200 Red Delicious apples before 2 p.m. If you can get the apples to him, he will pay you a dime for each apple. After thinking about it for a moment, you agree to get the apples for him and deliver them on time.

Here is your plan. There are plenty of Red Delicious apples on your trees. If you call some of your friends over, they can sit on the limbs and drop the apples for you to catch. If you pay them 3¢ for every apple they drop, you can make some money and get the apples to the store by 2 p.m.

This is a good plan if you can make it work. To make it work you will have to have a well-organized plan. You will have to put things in the right order. After reading this list, add some things that might have been overlooked, then place a number behind each item to indicate the order in which you would do it. The number "1" indicates the first thing you would do; "2" the second thing you would do, and so on for each item listed.

Processing: Call on students to read their "order of things" and justify items that have been added. Other students may be called upon to challenge the order of things presented.

Activity #26: The Right Order

Your neighbor is the manager of a supermarket. When he arrives home for lunch at 11:30 a.m., he tells you that he needs 200 Red Delicious apples before 2 p.m. If you can get the apples to him, he will pay you a dime for each apple. After thinking about it for a moment, you agree to get the apples for him and deliver them on time.

Here is your plan. There are plenty of Red Delicious apples on your trees. If you call some of your friends over, they can sit on the limbs and drop the apples for you to catch. If you pay them 3¢ for every apple they drop, you can make some money and get the apples to the store by 2 p.m.

This is a good plan if you can make it work. To make it work you will have to have a well-organized plan. You will have to put things in the right order. After reading this list, add some things that might have been overlooked, then place a number behind each item to indicate the order in which you would do it. The number "1" indicates the first thing you would do; "2" the second thing you would do, and so on for each item listed.

Eat my lunch.

_____   _____

Get a ladder.

_____   _____

Find some boxes.

_____   _____

Call some friends.

_____   _____

Pick out a tree.

_____   _____

Offer them 3¢ an apple.

_____   _____

_____   _____

_____   _____

_____   _____

Be prepared to explain your order of things.

Title: **Too Much of a Good Thing**

Teaching Target: To encourage students to think creatively in preparing to carry out their ideas. To provide an experience in planning and organizing. To provoke students and cause them to consider details of idea implementation.

Introduction: Have any of you ever eaten too much of anything like candy or pie? What happened? Maybe someone said that you had "too much of a good thing." When we get "fed up" with something, we are disturbed and bothered. We might decide to do something about it. We have an idea to solve our problem. Having an idea is not enough, there are other things we must do to solve our problem. Let's find out what they are.

Directions: Troy has a problem and an idea of how to fix it. Here's his story.

"When I leave my special ed class everyday, my special ed teacher usually gives me some extra work to take along. When I get back to my regular class I have to make up the work that I missed. I am also expected to do all of the homework that the other kids do. When I get home from my paper route my mom always has some chores for me to do. I never get to play, watch TV, or read sports magazines. All I do is work, work, work. I'm getting fed up with it. All of that work is too much of a good thing. I'm going to have a meeting and invite my mom, my classroom teacher, and my special ed teacher. We need to talk this over and see what can be done."

If Troy is to carry out his plan, he will have to give some thought to the details. Help Troy with the details by asking him some important questions.

Example: Where will you hold the meeting?

Processing: As needed, questioning may be conducted during the activity. Ask, "Have you thought about time, goals, drawbacks, when, where, your plan, information needed, who else might be involved, and what you want to have happen?"

If Troy has good answers to these questions, do you think his plan will work? Why or why not?

What advice would you give Troy before the meeting?

Activity #27: Too Much of a Good Thing

Troy has a problem and an idea of how to fix it. Here's his story.

"When I leave my special ed class everyday, my special ed teacher usually gives me some extra work to take along. When I get back to my regular class I have to make up the work that I missed. I am also expected to do all of the homework that the other kids do. When I get home from my paper route my mom always has some chores for me to do. I never get to play, watch TV, or read sports magazines. All I do is work, work, work. I'm getting fed up with it. All of that work is too much of a good thing. I'm going to have a meeting and invite my mom, my classroom teacher, and my special ed teacher. We need to talk this over and see what can be done."

If Troy is to carry out his plan, he will have to give some thought to the details. Help Troy with the details by asking him some important questions.

Example: Where will you hold the meeting?

1. _____

2. _____

3. _____

4. _____

5. _____

6. _____

7. _____

8. _____

9. _____

10. _____

If Troy has good answers to these questions, do you think his plan will work? Why or why not?

Title: Up a Tree

Teaching Target: To encourage students to "think it through" before acting on an idea. To cause students to consider difficulties that may arise in implementing an idea.

Introduction: There's a saying that goes something like this, "Even the best laid plans of mice and men sometimes goes awry." Who will explain what that means? At times, things do get messed up even when we take great pains to make them work out. But, things have a better chance of working out if we think things through and check out our plans before we move ahead. How do you go about checking out an idea? That's what we are going to do right now.

Directions: Suppose your cat was up in a tree and wouldn't come down. You want him to come down and have thought of some ways to solve the problem. Taking into consideration: a) your safety; b) the cat's safety; c) the time involved; and d) the cost involved, you have decided that No. 2 is your best solution. Before you go ahead with your plan, check it out by answering the questions in the right hand column.

Processing: Call on students to share their answers. Particularly ask if anyone has any other: **when, why, who, what, where,** and **how** questions.

After answering the check-out questions, do you still think that idea No. 2 is your best idea? Why do you think so?

Apply the checkout questions to other ideas listed, or to new and different ideas of your own.

Describe the advantages of "thinking through a problem."

Relate some experiences where problems were not "thought through."

In what ways is it a good idea to think about some possible difficulties you might encounter with a problem? How might this activity be helpful in solving problems of a different kind?

CPS For Kids

Activity #28: Up a Tree

Suppose your cat was up in a tree and wouldn't come down. You want him to come down and have thought of some ways to solve the problem. Taking into consideration: a) your safety; b) the cat's safety; c) the time involved; and d) the cost involved, you have decided that number 2 is your best solution. Before you go ahead with your plan, check it out by answering the questions in the right hand column.

My Ideas:

1. Climb the tree and get him myself.

2. Get a garden hose and sprinkle water on him.

3. Call the fire department to put up a ladder.

4. Call your dog and pet him. The cat will get jealous.

5. Forget the cat, he'll come down when he gets hungry.

After answering the checkout questions do you still think that idea No. 2 is your best idea? Why do you think so?

Apply the checkout questions to other ideas listed, or to new and different ideas of your own.

Checkout Questions:

1. **Who** should I tell about my plan?

_____

_____

2. **What** equipment will I need?

_____

_____

3. **When** should I go ahead with it?

_____

_____

4. **What** help will I need?

_____

_____

5. **Who** _____
_____?

6. **How** _____
_____?

7. **Where** _____
_____?

CPS For Kids **75**

Title: Battle of the Champions

Teaching Target: To engage students in analytical thinking for the purpose of considering why or how a plan might succeed or fail. To provide for the application of organizational and evaluative skills.

Introduction: I'm going to use some sentences to describe a situation. When I finish, I will ask you to tell all you can about the situation I describe. Here are the sentences:

> I wouldn't touch it.
> That's not my bag.
> I wouldn't get involved in that.
> I won't row that boat.
> Thanks, but no thanks.

(Conduct discussion on the situations described.)

There are times when someone has to get involved and make decisions, even if they are not popular with everyone. When this happens, you have to think it through and try to figure out how things will work out. Our work today calls on you to do these things: a) to figure things out; b) to make a plan; and c) to arrive at a decision about what to do.

Directions: Your city championship softball team is scheduled to play in the state tournament. If you can get by the first game, you have a good chance of winning the tournament. However, five of your players say they will quit the team if they don't get to start the game. As manager of the team you have some important decisions to make. Only four starting positions remain undecided.

After reading a description of the players in question, decide who will start the game. Write their names in the space provided. (Explain that there are six names that are to be written in the spaces.)

Processing: Call on students to explain why they made the decision to place certain individuals in the starting line-up. Probe student responses by asking **why** questions. Acknowledge creative, farsighted, well-organized responses.

Conduct a class consensus by asking students to vote on the players who should be in the starting line-up. Only four votes per student. Use the problem as a story starter. Have students write an account of how the state tournament turned out.

Activity #29: Battle of the Champions

Your city championship softball team is scheduled to play in the state tournament. If you can get by the first game, you have a good chance of winning the tournament. However, five of your players say they will quit the team if they don't get to start the game. As manager of the team you have some important decisions to make. Only four starting positions remain undecided.

Directions: After reading a description of the players in question, decide who will start the game. Write their names in the space provided.

Billy — best batter, has missed six games, plays the infield.

Mary Ann — only girl on the team, good outfielder, average batter, always on time, never misses a game.

Reggie — average batter, can play any position, wants to play the infield, Billy is his best friend.

Elroy — second best pitcher, won the championship game, can play the outfield, below average hitter.

Tommy — bats clean-up, good outfielder, teases Mary Ann, missed the championship game to go fishing.

You — manager of the team, an above average player, batting average .375, can play both infield and outfield.

_____ will start the game in the outfield.

_____ will start the game in the outfield.

_____ will start the game in the infield.

_____ will start the game in the infield.

_____ will not start the game.

_____ will not start the game.

At a team meeting, explain your decision for the starting line-up.

Title: Busy Bathroom

Teaching Target: To alert students to the conditions and reactions that may occur when they try to implement a new way of doing things. To impress upon students the need to prepare an implementation strategy.

Introduction: "Don't upset the apple cart" is a saying that people use when they don't want something to be changed. Have you asked yourself why people don't want things changed? Why don't they want the apple cart upset? What are your ideas about that? Can you think of some things that you didn't want to be changed? What were they? Today, our activity is about changing the way people do things, and the need to work out a plan.

Directions: Being the youngest in the family, you often find yourself "taking your turn" at the end of the morning line-up to use the bathroom. Your brothers, sisters, mom, and dad all want to get into the bathroom at the same time. To get to school on time, you often have to skip breakfast. Sometimes you are late. Let's say that you come up with this idea to solve the problem.

Brothers and sisters get up 15 minutes earlier and have five minutes each in the bathroom. Mom and Dad get up at the usual time and take 15 minutes. You get up 15 minutes later than usual and take whatever time you want. With this plan you also get to stay up 15 minutes longer to watch TV.

Now you have to get the others to accept your plan. What will you do? What will you say?

How will you get them to go along with your plan?

My plan is ...

Write your plan here.

Processing: This activity lends itself to role playing. Expect negative reactions to outweigh positive responses. Point out that negative responses may result as much from a poor implementation plan as well as unwelcomed ideas.

Students may be asked to suggest other ideas to solve the problem.

Activity #30: Busy Bathroom

Being the youngest in the family, you often find yourself "taking your turn" at the end of the morning line-up to use the bathroom. Your brothers, sisters, mom, and dad all want to get into the bathroom at the same time. To get to school on time, you often have to skip breakfast. Sometimes you are late. Let's say that you come up with this idea to solve the problem.

Brothers and sisters get up 15 minutes earlier and have five minutes each in the bathroom. Mom and Dad get up at the usual time and take 15 minutes. You get up 15 minutes later than usual and take whatever time you want. With this plan you also get to stay up 15 minutes longer to watch TV.

Now you have to get the others to accept your plan. What will you do? What will you say? How will you get them to go along with your plan?

My plan is ...

_____

_____

_____

_____

Write your plan here.

_____

_____

_____

_____

_____

Part IV

Worksheet Set for Individual or Group Problem-Solving

The following six reproducible worksheets provide a framework for solving different kinds of problems through Creative Problem-Solving.

Level I	Sensing Problems and Challenges
Level II	Fact Finding
Level III	Problem Finding
Level IV	Idea Finding
Level V	Solution Finding
Level VI	Acceptance Finding

Use this framework for ...

☞ A **School** Problem: "How can I improve my grades in science?"

☞ A **Home** Problem: "How can I get along better with my sister?"

☞ A **Thing** Problem: "How can I earn money for a vacation?"

And many, many other kinds of **Problems.**

Any of the 30 preceding activity pages may be duplicated for use in the classroom only. Permission to duplicate the activities and the following six worksheets is limited to use in the classroom.

Level I   CPS Worksheet No. 1

Sensing Problems and Challenges

What do you find confusing?

  What's messed up?

    What's bothering you?

      What would you like to do better?

        What do you want to improve?

  Tell your story. Describe the situation as you see it.

_____

_____

_____

_____

    What do you want to happen? Read your story, then tell what would make things better.

____   I want _____

____   I want _____

____   I want _____

____   I want _____

____   I want _____

Complete all of the above "I want" statements.
What do you really want to happen?
Place and "X" in front of the statement that tells what you want most.

CPS For Kids 81

Fact Finding

Below, write the "I want" statement you checked on Worksheet No. 1.

I want _____

Get the facts of your story on Worksheet No. 1 by answering these questions:

Who does this involve? _____

What has (or will) happened? _____

_____

When did it happen? _____

Where did it happen? _____

Why does this bother you? _____

Get more facts by asking and answering other **Who? What? When? Where? Why?** and **How?** questions. If needed, use another page.

_____

_____

_____

_____

_____

_____

The facts you have listed will help you to get at the problem or challenge that you have in mind. Read your "I want" statement at the top of this page. Do the facts suggest a different or more important problem or challenge? Should something else come first?

Level III   CPS Worksheet No. 3

Problem Finding

Check back to your "story" and "I want" statements on Worksheet No. 1. Compare this information with facts listed on Worksheet No. 2. Making whatever changes you wish, write your "I want" statement in the space below.

I want _____ .

Next, write questions about your "I want" statement to get at the problem or challenge. As indicated, all questions start with "How might I?" Use all of the spaces.

Example: How might I get kids to like me?

___ How might I _____ ?

___ How might I _____ ?

___ How might I _____ ?

Now, for each of the above questions, ask, "Why do I want to do this?" Take the answer and make up another question that starts with, "In what ways might I?"

Example: In what ways might I make more friends?

___ In what ways might I _____ ?

___ In what ways might I _____ ?

___ In what ways might I _____ ?

Read all of your questions. Place an "X" in front of the question that really gets at your problem or challenge.

Level IV   CPS Worksheet No. 4

Idea Finding

Write the "What ways?" statement that you checked on Worksheet No. 3.

_____

_____

List ideas to answer your "What ways?" question: (Far out ideas are OK).

— _____   — _____

— _____   — _____

— _____   — _____

— _____   — _____

— _____   — _____

Use the *Scamper* checklist to get ideas. If needed, use another page.

S   Substitute what?
C   Combine what?
A   Adapt, make it fit.
M   Modify, magnify, minify what?
P   Put it to other uses.
E   What else? Who else?
R   Reverse or rearrange what?

Next, place an "X" in front of the five ideas that offer the best solution to your problem or challenge. Write them in spaces A-E on Worksheet No. 5.

Level V   CPS Worksheet No. 5

Solution Finding

First: In spaces A-E, write the ideas you selected on Worksheet No. 4.

Second: List the measures you will use to judge your ideas in spaces 1-5.

Third: With reference to Measure No. 1, compare all ideas and award points.

Fourth: Continue to award points for each measure before going to the next idea.

Idea Rating Scale

Points: 1 - Poor   2 - Below Average   3 - Average   4 - Good   5 - Excellent

MEASURES to see how good your ideas are.	Creative Ideas				
	A.	B.	C.	D.	E.
1.					
2.					
3.					
4.					
5.					
Total Points					

Down the page, add points for each idea and enter the total in the space provided. Compare the total points for each idea. Continue with Worksheet No. 6.

Level VI   CPS Worksheet No. 6

Acceptance Finding

My problem: Write the "What ways?" statement you checked on Worksheet No. 3.

_____

My idea: Write the idea, or combination of ideas, selected on Worksheet No. 5.

_____

Thinking it through: Before writing your plan, think it through by asking:

Who needs to know about it?
When should I get started?
Why is this the best idea?
What materials will I need?
Where will there be opposition?

My plan: In order, list what you will do to put your plan to work. If needed, use another page.

_____

_____

_____

_____

_____

_____

_____

_____

Now, put your plan to work by doing the things you have listed. As you move ahead, be on the lookout for other things that need to be improved.

Bibliography

Bingham, Alma, *Improving Children's Facility in Problem-Solving*. New York, NY: Bureau of Publications, Teachers College, Columbia University, 1963.

Biondi, Angelo M., ed., *Have an Affair with Your Mind*. Great Neck, NY: Creative Synergetic Association, 1974.

Biondi, Angelo M., ed., *The Creative Process*. Buffalo, NY: D.O.K. Publishers, 1973.

Cole, Henry P., *Process Education*. Englewood Cliffs, NJ: Educational Technology Publications, 1972.

Davis, Gary, *Psychology of Problem Solving: Theory and Practice*. New York, NY: Basic Books, 1973.

Davis, G., and Scott, J., eds., *Training Creative Thinking*. New York, NY: Holt, Rinehart and Winston, 1971.

DeBono, Edward, *Children Solve Problems*. New York, NY: Harper and Row, 1972.

DeBono, Edward, *Lateral Thinking, Creativity Step by Step*. New York, NY: Harper and Row, 1973.

DeRoche, Edward F., *Creative Problem-Solving Techniques for Elementary School Teachers and Children*. New York, NY: Carlton Press, 1968.

Eberle, Bob, *Scamper: Games for Imagination and Development*. Waco, TX: Prufrock Press, 1996.

Eberle, Bob, and Hall, Rosie, *Affective Direction: Planning and Teaching for Thinking and Feeling*. Buffalo, NY: D.O.K. Publishers, 1979.

Feldhusen, J.F., and Treffinger, D.J., *Teaching Creative Thinking and Problem Solving*. Dubuque: Kendall-Hunt, 1977.

Gowan, John Curtis, *Development of the Creative Individual*. San Diego: Knapp Publishers, 1972.

Gowan, John C., *Trance, Art and Creativity*. Buffalo, NY: The Creative Education Foundation, 1975.

Guilford, J.P., *The Nature of Human Intelligence*, New York: McGraw-Hill, 1967.

Hudgins, Bryce B., *Problem Solving in the Classroom*. New York: MacMillan, 1966.

Koberg, Don and Bagnall, Jim, *The Universal Traveler*. Los Altos, CA: William Kaufman, Inc., 1972.

MacKinnon, Donald W., *In Search of Human Effectiveness, Identifying and Developing Creativity*. Buffalo, NY: The Creative Education Foundation, 1978.

McKim, Robert H., *Experiences in Visual Thinking*. Belmont, CA: Brooks/Cole Publishing Co., 1972.

Noller, Ruth B., *Scratching the Surface of Creative Problem-Solving, A Bird's Eye View of CPS*. Buffalo, NY: D.O.K. Publishers, 1977.

Noller, Ruth B., Treffinger, Donald J., and Houseman, Elwood D., *It's a Gas to be Gifted* or *CPS for the Gifted and Talented*. Buffalo, NY: D.O.K. Publishers, 1977.

Noller, Ruth B., Parnes, Sidney J., and Biondi, Angelo M., *Creative Actionbook*. New York, NY: Charles Scribner's Sons, 1976.

Osborn, Alex F., *Applied Imagination*. New York, NY: Charles Scribner's Sons, 1963.

Parnes, Sidney J., *Aha, Insights Into Creative Behavior*. Buffalo, NY: D.O.K. Publishers, 1975.

Parnes, Sidney J., Noller, Ruth B., and Biondi, Angelo M., *Guide to Creative Action*. New York, NY: Charles Scribner's Sons, 1976.

Stanish, Bob, *I Believe in Unicorns: Classroom Experiences for Activating Creative Thinking*. Carthage, IL: Good Apple, Inc., 1979.

Stanish, Bob, *Sunflowering: Thinking, Feeling, Doing Activities for Creative Expression*. Carthage, IL: Good Apple, Inc., 1977.

Torrance, E. Paul, *The Search for Satori and Creativity*. Buffalo, NY: The Creative Education Foundation, 1979.

Torrance, E. Paul, *Guiding Creative Talent*. Englewood Cliffs, NJ: Prentice-Hall, 1962.

Torrance, E. Paul, *Rewarding Creative Behavior*. Englewood Cliffs, NJ: Prentice-Hall, 1965.

Torrance, E. Paul, and Meyers, Robert E., *Creative Learning and Teaching*. New York, NY: Harper and Row, 1970.

References

Eberle, Robert F., *Scamper: Games for Imagination and Development.* Waco, TX: Prufrock Press, 1996.

Eberle, Robert F., *Scamper On: Games for Imagination and Development.* Waco, TX: Prufrock Press, 1996.

Elwell, Patricia A., and Treffinger, Donald J., eds., *CPS for Teens.* Waco, TX: Prufrock Press, 1993.

Maslow, Abraham H., *The Farther Reaches of Human Nature.* New York, NY: The Viking Press, 1971.

McIntosh, Joel E., and Meacham, April W., *Creative Problem Solving in the Classroom.* Waco, TX: Prufrock Press, 1992.

Noller, Ruth B., Parnes, Sidney J., and Biondi, Angelo M., *Creative Actionbook.* New York, NY: Charles Scribner's Sons, 1976.

Noller, Ruth B., *Scratching the Surface of Creative Problem-Solving, A Bird's Eye View of CPS.* Buffalo, NY: D.O.K. Publishers, 1977.

Osborn, Alex F., *Applied Imagination.* New York, NY: Charles Scribner's Sons, 1967.

Parnes, Sidney J., *Creative Behavior Guidebook.* New York, NY: Charles Scribner's Sons, 1967.

Stanish, Bob, and Eberle, Robert F., *Be A Problem-Solver.* Waco, TX: Prufrock Press, 1996.

Torrance, E. Paul, *Guiding Creative Talent.* Englewood Cliffs, NJ: Prentice-Hall, 1962.

Vincent, William S., *Indicators of Quality, Signs of Good Teaching.* New York, NY: Institute of Administrative Research, Columbia University, 1969.